Warren's World

BY WARREN MILLER

MOUNTAIN SPORTS PRESS

Boulder, Colorado

Warren's World
© 2002 Warren Miller

Printed in the United States of America.

ISBN 0-9676747-8-6

Library of Congress Cataloging-in-Publication data applied for.

First printing, June 2002

Front cover photograph by Jack Affleck.

Some of the stories included in this book have previously appeared in numerous publications over the years. Unfortunately, the names of a few of those publications have dribbled out of my memory bank over time. Here is a partial list of those I do remember: *SKI Magazine, The Aspen Times, Rocky Mountain News, Wood River Journal, Anacortes American, Lone Peak Lookout, DenverNewsDaily.com, Mammoth Times, Reno Air,* and various Lake Tahoe newspapers. A few of them have also appeared in my previous books, *Wine, Women, Warren & Skis, On Film In Print, In Search of Skiing,* and *Lurching from One Near Disaster to the Next.*

Publisher/Editor-in-Chief: Bill Grout
Associate Publisher: Alan Stark
Art Director/Designer: Michelle Klammer Schrantz
Associate Art Director: Scott Kronberg
Managing Editor: Chris Salt
Sales Representative: Andy Hawk

A subsidiary of:

MOUNTAIN SPORTS PRESS

929 Pearl Street, Suite 200
Boulder, CO 80302
303-448-7617

TABLE OF

IN SEARCH OF THE FREE LIFT TICKET

How Cold Was It? 2

My Diary 10

Parking Lot Cuisine 17

Leftover Chicken Legs 24

The Parking Lot Ski Team 32

Moguls and Michelangelo 39

Two Girls, A Frozen Buick and Homemade
    Ice Cream at Eight Below Zero 48

Taking It Straight 55

The Girl and the DC-3 61

Renegade Instructor 66

Laces and Koogi Ties 72

Squaw Valley, 1950: A Season of Firsts 88

FIFTY YEARS WITH SKIS AND CAMERA

The Education of a Filmmaker 96

How to Become an Overnight Success .101

The Way it Was 104

Skid Chains 109

Dinner with the Governor 112

Fingerprints on the Tram 117

Cathedral of the Gods 121

The Killy Caper, Part 1 126

The Killy Caper, Part 2 131

Hot Dog Roast 136

My Father Hates You 140

CONTENTS

STRANGE BUT TRUE

Science Comes to Skiing 146

Monkeying Around on Skis 149

My Second Day on Skis 152

A Shortcut to Fame 158

Chairlift Lines 161

A Day of Skiing for $1.75 168

Lifts Long Forgotten 172

What the Shah Didn't Know 175

Mysterious Ernest 179

The Antelope Who Loved Cigarette Butts 183

Those Crafty French 186

Impasse in a Crevasse 190

SHORT SWINGS

Freedom 196

Christmas 199

Buzzwords 204

Don't Keep Score 208

Get In Shape 211

The Presidential Ski Weekend 215

Insecurities List 219

What Happened to The Entrepreneurs? 222

Reality Check 226

The Good Old Days 230

INTRODUCTION

I n 1933, with the month's wages that I'd saved from my 10-cents-a-Saturday job at the neighborhood grocery store, I walked into the Sontag drugstore in Hollywood, California, and told the clerk, "I want to buy that camera in the showcase."

That 35-cent camera with "sports viewfinder" turned out to be the most important purchase I ever made in my life. Two years after the purchase of that Univex camera, I spent some time in the Boy Scouts, where I used the camera to start one of my first entrepreneurial ventures—selling pictures of our hiking trips to other scouts. That in turn led to a lifetime of never having to work for a living. Instead of working, I spent all day, every day, all winter, skiing or filming other skiers. During the summer, when the surf wasn't up, I glued the film together that I had shot during the winter months and then, during the gray days of October, November and December, I traveled from town to town to show the film and narrate it live, while hoping to sell enough tickets to make my next movie.

Sometimes, when the weather didn't cooperate during the winter, I had to hang around resorts such as Chamonix, Mammoth, Zermatt, Mt. Cook, Zurs, Sun Valley, Vail or Whistler for as long as a week with nothing to do. During that time I just skied in the deep powder snow while I waited for the sun to come out so I could take movies of yet another ski resort. There were days when the sunshine, skiers, snow and mountains truly became a "symphony on skis."

In 1950, the year I showed my first ski movie in the Sun Valley Opera House, only a handful of people showed up. After the show, the theatre manager told me, "Always entertain the people who show up and feel sorry for the ones that don't." With that bit of advice, we split the $37 in ticket sales for the evening. I got 40 percent or $14.80, which was enough to buy gas for me to get to my next show.

In 1990, after 40 years on the road showing my feature length ski films, I was offered a job writing a weekly column for a ski resort newspaper

for $10 a week. The editor told me to just write stories about things that had happened to me—but had never made it into my movies. Now here I am, many years and tens of thousands of words later, gathering up some of those columns from the dozen or so newspapers—and the two national magazines—that have published my writings, and with the help of the folks at Mountain Sports Press, gluing them together into this book.

After 65 years on skis, I still ski about a hundred days a winter, and if I live to be 123 I might be able to shoot my age on a golf course. But I usually don't keep score, because I've always believed in freedom-oriented sports where there is no score, where there is no winner or loser, where everyone who participates is the winner.

One question I am often asked is, "When are you going to retire?" Since I never have worked, what is there to retire from? There are always more mountains to be skied, more trips to take in our boat, more stories to write about my life spent lurching from one near disaster to the next— which is the real story of my life together with my great wife Laurie.

—Warren Miller
Deer Harbor, Washington
June 2002

IN SEARCH OF THE
FREE LIFT TICKET

How Cold Was It?

O n this particular below-zero night in February 1947, the four of us were hunkered down under thick blankets in a horse-drawn sleigh with about 20 other couples. We were on our way back to the Sun Valley Lodge after a steak dinner and dancing at Trail Creek Cabin. Above us, in the clear black winter sky, Orion stood out prominently among two hundred billion zillion other stars. Give or take a few.

The rusty metal that held the elderly pieces of the wooden hay wagon together creaked in the cold as the wagon twisted and bent while its runners slid over the ruts, dips and rises of the well-traveled path back to Sun Valley. The team of big draft horses was almost hidden in a cloud of steam as they pulled us home.

"Whoa!"

The big hay wagon groaned to a stop, and then, one by one, the couples untangled themselves from the blankets, the straw and each other, feeling the aches and pains from the first three days of their ski vacations.

My friend Ward Baker and I helped our dates climb down from the wagon, and we started slowly walking back to the Lodge with them.

I should clarify something here. They were not really our dates; they were our escorts. Ward had met both of them at lunch in the Roundhouse two days before as they were finishing up their cheese-burgers, fries, rootbeer and apple pie à la mode, and we were finishing up our daily soup made from free-for-the-taking oyster crackers and Ketchup in hot water.

Ward introduced me to the girls when he discovered that we had a lot in common—all of us were from California. To Ward this was

enough common ground to invite both of them for an after-lunch ski
run down College. In those days, College was the only semi-easy run on
Baldy and an ideal trail to find out if someone was a good enough skier
to bother spending the rest of the day with. If not, you could always
turn right down another trail and lose them.

These ladies were both good skiers. Born and raised in San
Francisco, they had learned to ski at Yosemite and had mastered the
snowplow and the stem turn, and they could even do an occasional
stem christie. Even though this was our first full winter on skis, Ward
and I were already fans of the radically different French Ski

Technique—no stem, no snowplowing, just parallel turns based on side-slipping. And we were more than willing to teach the girls what we thought was a more effective technique.

Skiing down College, the four of us stopped often and talked a lot. After four stops, Ward selected the pretty blonde for his pupil. This was fine by me, because I thought the brunette was the real charmer anyway.

Over the next 10 minutes, I found out that she was studying structural engineering at Berkeley. Her father was an attorney, she had two brothers named George and Robert, a dog named Studley, a cat named Desirable, a membership in the St. Francis Yacht Club where her father raced his 40-foot something or other, a summer home at Stinson Beach, and she drove a Buick as I did. Because of all of this inside information and her engineering background, it was easy for me to explain the French Ski Technique. I talked about force vectors, inertia, centrifugal force, up unweighting and lateral heel displacement by transferring rotational energy to the skis with simultaneous contraction of the legs using a method called ruade. She just nodded her head as though she understood what ruade really meant and continued right on making her turns in a very wide snowplow.

To someone watching us teach these two pretty ladies to ski, it would appear that we were hustling them. We were. However, hustling means different things to different people. When you live in a snow-covered eight-foot-long trailer without heat or electricity, as we did, hustling means simply lining up dates who were paying Lodge guests so we could spend as much time as possible sitting by the Lodge fireplace soaking up heat.

By the third run, our two pupils offered to trade us a pair of dinners at Trail Creek Cabin for the ski lessons we were giving them. This would be an expensive evening: Five dollars a person for the round-trip sleigh ride, all the hors d'oeuvres you could eat and a big steak dinner. Drinks were extra, but since none of us were drinkers, Ward and I figured we could at least buy a few rounds of Coca Cola or rootbeer, even though Coca Cola cost 20 cents a glass.

After the sleigh ride, we walked into the Lodge and up to the Redwood Room where a big fire was burning. I was pleased to find that we had the room all to ourselves. Our pre-arranged plan was to sit around the fireplace making polite conversation for at least 30 minutes. This would let us soak up as much heat as possible before we would have to slink back to our below zero trailer in the parking lot.

Nothing is forever. As Ward and I babbled on about metal edges and bindings, rotational energy, torsional rigidity of a laminated ski and its relationship to the fall line, our two escorts fell asleep. One of the ladies sat slack-jawed and limp on the big couch, while the other had slumped over in a big easy chair and was sawing Zs just as enthusiastically.

Since conversation was at an end, Ward and I went back downstairs, across the lobby and out to our trailer, which was parked about 200 yards from the front door of the Lodge, way over in the far corner of the parking lot under a stand of aspens. The thermometer outside the Lodge front door registered 31 degrees below zero. There were still six or seven more hours of darkness, and we knew from experience that the temperature could drop another five or six degrees before morning.

It takes almost as long to explain the ritual that was necessary for us to get into bed in our tiny trailer as it did to perform it. On nights like this, when we had our best clothes on, it took even longer.

Ward always got into bed first, because he slept farthest from the door. After he was in bed, I would straighten out my two army surplus down sleeping bags that were inside of each other, then unzip them both so they would be ready for me to eventually, gingerly, and as soon as possible, ease down into.

Next I would stand by the right rear door of our Buick convertible that was parked in front of the trailer. I would unzip my parka but leave it on. Then I would untie my necktie, unbutton my dress shirt, and then in one swift motion shrug out of my parka, my tweed sport coat, my dress shirt, my necktie and my T-shirt. Then, standing there naked from the waist up, I would drape all of them over the same coat hanger, hang them in the back of the car and pull on my frozen-stiff sweatshirt that I used for a pajama top. So far so good.

The hard part was getting my bottom half ready for bed.

On this particular night, I removed my pants, shoes, socks and underwear and was standing there, my bottom half stark naked, while I balanced precariously on the one foot that I'd just inserted into my navy flight boot. Suddenly I was illuminated by a pair of headlights. A couple had been messing around in a nearby car, heard the commotion of me undressing, and switched on their lights to see what was going on.

What can you do in a situation like this?

Just wave hello!

I finished waving and got my right leg into my freezing-cold long johns. Then, as I was raising my left leg and inserting it into the other long john leg, I started to fall. Grabbing the door handle, I managed to yank the car door open and three weeks' worth of frozen, dirty laundry poured out on top of me as I fell. Sitting there on the ice, my naked fanny quick-freezing to the icy parking lot, it took less than three-sixteenths of a second before I had that long underwear on and yanked up almost to my throat.

Easing my bare foot into my other flight boot, I stuffed the three weeks' worth of frozen-together dirty clothes back into the car, then shuffled back to the trailer door. Ward was already snoring.

Sitting down on the edge of the bed with my feet outside the door, I slid my feet out of the flight boots and ooched my fanny into the center of my half of the bed. Now I had to find out where the sleeping bag zippers were and try to fit my legs down inside of both sleeping bags without the icy metal zippers touching any part of my body. Usually there was still some frost left around the opening of the sleeping bag from my breathing that had condensed and frozen the night before, so I always had to be careful not to drag any of it inside the bag with me.

It always took three or four minutes to get my legs, up to the knees, down into the bag and to warm up that part of it. Then I worked my way down inside the bag up to the waist. And so it went, up to my armpits, then up to my shoulders, and finally up to my neck. By then I had used up so much heat to warm up the bag that I had to lay in a fetal position for 10 or 15 minutes before I could straighten out. It was at least 20 minutes after the whole going-to-bed ritual had started before I was undressed, in bed, straightened out, zipped up, warmed up and nodding off to sleep.

On this particular night, we were quite comfortable lying there, snug in our sleeping bags. I gazed out the open door at the Lodge in the near distance. Ward and I didn't envy the Lodge guests whatsoever. Except for heat, we had everything those Lodge guests had—and a lot more, too. We were skiing every day, all day, all winter, and they were only in Sun Valley for a week. They had to get back to their obligations. We had none. We weren't concerned about status, money, a house, a wife, kids or new cars. We had other, more important things to learn.

Such as how not to freeze to death in the Sun Valley Lodge parking lot every night.

On nights when it was below zero, our breath would freeze and attach itself to the ceiling and walls of our trailer. On a really cold night, the ceiling would get so much frozen vapor stuck to it that our breath would begin to float back down in the form of miniature snowflakes, coating the area around the tops of our sleeping bags.

We learned very quickly that anything with moisture on it that didn't go into our sleeping bags with us would be frozen as hard as the aluminum sides of our trailer by morning. Ski pants, socks, sweaters, boots, parkas, gloves, you name it; if it wasn't brand spanking clean, it would always be frozen. Sometimes a garment would even freeze to the inside wall of the trailer, right where we had discarded it when we went to bed. Whatever piece of clothing destined for our warm bodies in the morning had to be put inside our sleeping bags at night.

There was a limit, however, to the number of pieces of clothing and other stuff we could cram into the bottom of our sleeping bag and still have room for our not-yet-frozen bodies. If we filled them up too much and turned over during the night, what we had in the bottom of our bag wouldn't turn over. Then the opening at the top of the mummy bag where our heads stuck out would tighten around our necks. More than once I woke up gagging and screaming for air with frost around my face and in my ears and hair.

I had hair then.

Naturally, this made it very difficult to go back to sleep very quickly. If it was already gray in the East, I would get up and go for my morning walk over to the Skier's Chalet.

While it might appear that getting up was harder than going to bed, it really wasn't. When I came down off the mountain in the afternoon, I usually hung up my ski pants, sweater and socks at the foot of the bed. So, in the morning I could just sit up, unzip both sleeping bags, put my sweater on and then, twisting my body 90 degrees, I would stick my legs outside of the trailer while still encased in the sleeping bags. Then I would ease them out of the mummy bags and climb into my freezing-cold pants. I had to be careful to keep my bare feet off the ice beside the trailer, pull on my socks, then my flight boots, grab my shaving kit and ski boots, and amble over to the Skier's Chalet for my morning shower and shave.

The only time that getting my pants on presented a problem was when it was snowing hard and I had to get into them while still lying in bed. When I did this, I would always arrive at the Skier's Chalet with duck feathers all over my pants. On snowy mornings, there were never any paying guests in the showers that early, so feather-covered pants and sweaters were no big deal.

While showering and shaving, I would set my ski boots on top of the radiator, and they would be thawed out and toasty warm by the time I finished.

Oh, yes, I would also bring along whatever was left of our frozen milk so I could thaw it out for our daily ration of hot oatmeal. I would also bring along the pan to cook the oatmeal in and fill it up with warm water before going back to the trailer to start cooking breakfast.

"Sequence of events," the time and motion study analysts call it. Ward and I really got really good at this going-to-bed sequence of events. Of course, our most important sequence of events occurred when were sneaking onto the ski lift first thing in the morning so we could get first tracks in all the new powder snow.

Sometimes, with this constant battle for survival in subarctic conditions, we just didn't have the energy to hustle a date so we could sit in front of the Lodge fireplace and soak up heat. But we were always available to trade ski lessons for a hot meal.

If the pupil asked first.

My Diary

March 17, 1947

Food, Silt, Colorado, Warren, 76 cents

Gas, Fruita, Colorado, Warren, 13.3 gals $3.20

Up early to find Ward has parked us on the main street of Silt. Curious people keep peering in, so we get up and leave. Breakfast beside the road. Shotgun loaded but no game seen. Warren driving. Hits chickens out of Grand Junction, but nearness of farmer prohibits us from having a good dinner. Milkshake in Fruita, Colorado.

Gas $3.49, Provo, Food $5.03. Hunting but no game sighted. Later try it but wind up stuck in soft shoulder. Truck rescues us. On up to Alta and dinner of steaks. Bed early.

This diary was written in smudged lead pencil (the events happened before the invention of the ballpoint pen) in a tattered spiral notebook that I have somehow managed to keep in my library for the last 55 years. I wrote the diary in the front seat of the Buick while tootling down the highway, or under the brilliance of our Coleman lantern while one of us was cooking dinner, or in the parking lots of some of the finest ski resorts in the West.

Let me fill in between the lines:

Food, Silt, Colorado, 76 cents.

That would be for a large box of oatmeal, a loaf of bread, a quart of milk, oleomargarine and peanut butter, which would round out the 76-cent grocery bill. This formed the mainstay of our well-balanced, something-from-nearly-every-food-group diet.

Up early to find that Ward has parked us on the main street of Silt, Colorado.

It was Saturday morning in Silt, and we had overslept. The night before we had driven the 80 some miles on a narrow two-land road from Aspen. For no reason at all our headlights had started going off randomly. The Buick had a mind of its own as far as lighting our way at night was concerned, so we usually tried to find a good campsite before dark. In fact, the headlights had gone out between Aspen and Glenwood Springs just as we spotted a deer. Unfortunately, someone else hadn't spotted it soon enough and had center punched it with the radiator. It lay dead and still bleeding beside the road when we drove up and stopped. With the thought of barbecued venison steaks dancing in our heads, we were hunkered down beside it trying to figure out exactly how to butcher it when a car coming the other way swerved over the double line and skidded to a halt in front of us. Our usual good luck had attracted the local sheriff on his once-a-week inspection of this part of his territory.

"No, boys, I wouldn't recommend you cut any steaks from this one. Something about their adrenalin spoiling the meat when they get killed this way."

Heading west from Glenwood Springs, we drove part of the way to Silt in total darkness because of our going-out-on-their-own headlights. The buildings in Silt were the first we had seen in over an hour, so we parked on the leeward side of one of them.

Now that I've explained why we arrived late in Silt, and why we were very tired when we decided on this location, you'll understand what follows.

Before going to bed, we usually just dumped all of our junk that was inside the trailer outside. The big pile of parkas, ski pants, a couple of extra sleeping bags, Ward's 65 feet of inch-and-a-half manila hemp mooring line/tow rope, a Coleman lantern and a shovel or two made a pile three feet high and about six feet in diameter. The pile was right in the middle of what turned out to be the sidewalk in front of the general store.

The farmers and ranchers who had driven into town for their early Saturday morning shopping had been climbing around and over our accumulation of junk. It was spring and warm by our standards, so we had the trailer door wide open.

I was still half asleep when I heard the murmur of voices, "There has to be someone in there, or else there's been an awful wreck here. But the car doesn't look too damaged, just kinda old."

"Yeah! And really smelly and dirty."

I was afraid to move, or open my eyes. I was trying to nudge Ward when there was a great banging on the roof of the trailer. It sounded like metal against metal. We both sat up instantly as a 52-inch waistline blotted out the sun streaming in through our bedroom door. My first thought as I gazed at the fat form was, "They couldn't possibly make Levis that big."

I knew that the owner of that waistline couldn't bend over, but as he awkwardly tried to peer into our bedroom, a humongously large six-shooter glinted in the morning sun.

"O.K. boys. Let's get this garbage picked up right now, and I want you two and this wreck out of town before I finish my cup of coffee. And I'll tell you that my morning coffee takes about a half an hour. Do I make myself clear?"

"Yes, sir, Mister Sheriff! We understand. We have no problem with that."

Under normal circumstances it usually took us at least an hour to get out of bed, get all our stuff sorted out and dumped back into the trailer, get the car started and be on our way. This time we accomplished all of the above, bought gas and groceries and were out of the city limits of Silt, Colorado, long before the sheriff finished his morning coffee.

Ten miles down the road, after checking our rearview mirror every 500 yards or so, we found a place to pull off and make a pot of our wonderful, soon-to-be-patented oatmeal. It was wonderful, filled us up, warmed us up and, most important, it was cheap.

"Your child will ski as well as you do for one day in your life. The next day they'll ski better."

So why not patent it?

It was only about two cents a bowl.

Dishes washed and put away, I took the morning driving shift, and we commiserated with each other about the fact that all of the ski lifts would stop running and the ski season would end in three or four weeks. Ergo, no more ski season for us. We were cruising along, planning the last month of our winter when, just out of Grand Junction, I had the best opportunity ever to gather up a great dinner at no cost whatsoever. At least 30 chickens where scratching and pecking in the shoulder of the highway up ahead.

I gunned the engine and got the tired Buick and trailer up to almost 40 miles an hour. Those chickens must have heard us coming, because they started scattering every which way. I plotted my interception trajectory as I factored in my directional angle and lineal speed in relation to the rapidly accelerating chickens in order to nail at least a couple of them. Focused intently on the rapidly scattering herd of chickens, I skidded across what turned out to be about half an acre of freshly planted farmhouse lawn until I finally nailed two of them with my front bumper.

That was when Ward hollered, "Miller, you just missed that farmer's front porch. You put big grooves through his newly planted lawn, and I think that's his wife coming out the front door with what looks like a shotgun. I'd suggest we don't even slow down. Let's pass on the chicken dinner and get out of here."

Ward was looking at the front porch and didn't see the farmer racing his tractor across the barnyard toward us at a rate of speed that tractors are not designed to travel. I floored the Buick and with the trailer full of ski stuff fishtailing across his new front and side yard, we got out of there. I swerved left to avoid a broadside collision with the tractor as a roar of his wife's shotgun was followed by a few shotgun pellets hitting the rear of our car and trailer. They had little effect, however, because by this time we were going the same direction and about the same speed as the pellets.

Hunting but no game sighted. Later try it but wind up stuck in a soft shoulder. Truck rescues us. On up to Alta and dinner of steaks. Bed early.

"No game sighted" means we walked and walked and walked but didn't sight anything except three scraggly cattle, five deer and a covey of quail, none of which we could get close enough to hit with our .410 shotgun or our bent-barrel .22 caliber rifle.

When we finally got back to the car, we discovered what those yellow signs beside the road meant when they said: "Soft Shoulder." The Buick had slowly sunk up to its axles. The shoulder had been frozen rock hard for the last three months, but in the hot spring sun the final inch or so of permafrost had melted, and we were stuck big time. As we approached the car, the Utah gumbo that the highway contractor had used to build the roadbed sucked our flight boots off with each step we took.

We finally had to leave our flight boots where they were, roll up our pants, wade through the ankle-deep gunk and get the shovels and start digging. One of us would dig while the other went out to the nearby hardpan and started gathering up brush and twigs to somehow make a roadbed so we could eventually drive out of this gunk. We also had to put on skid chains. Putting on skid chains in a muddy bog like this can dramatically alter your appreance. After we had finished the trench that we dug in the front of the car, we were muddy from head to toe.

We were almost ready to start trying to drive our car out when a state highway dump truck stopped on the nearby asphalt and offered to tow us. We used Ward's one-and-one-half-inch manila mooring line/tow rope. That dump truck yanked us out of that mud as easily as sucking a chocolate shake through a straw. Then the driver slammed on his brakes while we skidded on our muddy bald tires and narrowly averted squashing the hood of the car under the bed of the truck. I had to swerve over the double line to miss it, and an on-coming car had to swerve into the shoulder to miss us. Now the dump truck had to turn around and pull that car out.

The dump truck driver borrowed our muddy mooring line and so we had to sit around and wait. When he returned the rope, he said, "I leased them the rope for five dollars, so here's your half of it."

We were finally on our way, $2.50 richer and 900 pounds of Utah mud heavier. As Ward began to pick up speed there was a terrible racket. We didn't have fenders on the trailer, so all that mud that was stuck to the wheels was being spun off to land on the back of the car.

Not to worry. It looked like rain up ahead, and all the mud would be washed off. It was. Except when we hit that spring rainstorm we discovered all the places that our convertible top had ripped or split during the winter. So we got the mud off the outside of the car but wound up with about 11 gallons of water and 39 pounds of mud in the car.

It was feast or famine, usually a lot more of the latter than the former.

Parking Lot Cuisine

fter camping out in the Alta, Utah, parking lot for eight days, our tiny trailer buried under newly fallen snow, Ward Baker and I had just about run out of money. We were camping there because Alta boasted three of the 12 chairlifts in America at the time. (One of them would be demolished by an avalanche a month or so after we left, and then there would be 11 chairlifts in America.)

The Number One chairlift was similar to a mine tram built to carry ore buckets. It had a fixed cable from the top terminal to the bottom, stretched between wooden towers that looked like telephone poles. Underneath the fixed cable was a moving cable that had individual chairs fastened to it. Each chair hung from a pair of grooved metal wheels that ran on the fixed cable above. The noise of those metal wheels on the steel cable was so loud you could hear the chairlift five miles down the canyon. It cost $2.50 a day to ride this and the other two chairlifts at Alta. Each of the three chairlifts had a capacity of about 300 people an hour. On weekends, carloads of skiers drove up from nearby Salt Lake City, creating liftlines as long as 45 minutes.

Ward and I had been paying for lift tickets for the past eight days and now were getting desperate for lift-ticket money. Since we didn't want to stand in long liftlines on the weekends, we decided to look for weekend jobs so we could ski during the week. I had learned as a kid during the Depression to always look for work in the food services industry, because that also meant free meals.

We soon found jobs cooking hamburgers on weekends at the Snowpine Lodge. We were paid 50 cents an hour for a 10-hour shift—or $5 a day and all the hamburgers we could eat. By Sunday night we would

There sat the Buick convertible and the eight-foot trailer under a foot-and-a-half of snow.

have earned $10 each, enough to pay for the next four days of skiing.

The Snowpine Lodge was located at the very end of the narrow road up Little Cottonwood Canyon, miraculously situated right between two deadly avalanche paths. The lodge had a flat roof so that in the event a big avalanche came roaring down it would slide right over the building and take out the front porch.

But the lodge turned out to be a nice warm laid-back place to work for a couple of frozen parking-lot residents. In the first few hours of our job, we learned to accidentally drop a raw hamburger patty or a bun on the floor every so often. Of course, we couldn't sell a dirty hamburger to a paying customer. Instead, we would pick it up, along with the paper napkin we had dropped it in, and throw it into the "trash" at the bottom of our rucksack. I had taken differential and integral calculus courses in college, so it was very easy for me to extrapolate exactly how many hamburger patties to drop on the floor. We'd need enough meat for all our dinners from Monday through Friday—an even dozen, I calculated.

But by Wednesday we'd have to gradually start adding rice to our meatloaf or stew to make up for the dwindling supply of hamburger. For variety we would occasionally savor one of the few remaining goat-meat chops that Ward had brought from Catalina Island.

Before joining me as a resident of the Alta parking lot, Ward Baker had been a commercial fisherman, sailing out of Southern California and doing most of his fishing around nearby Catalina Island. Catalina was overrun with wild goats, thousands and thousands of them busy making thousands and thousands more. The goats could always be seen scrambling around on the steep cliffs that rose up out of the Pacific, and they paid very little attention to any boat that might happen by.

From the deck of his rocking and rolling fishing boat, even without benefit of ballistic trajectory analysis, it was easy for Ward to fire his single-shot, bent-barrel .22-caliber rifle in their general direction. When he occasionally managed to hit one, the goat would roll and bounce down the cliff until it finally splashed into the ocean. Then Ward would stow his rifle, launch his dinghy and row to the dead goat while it was still floating. He had to get there before the blood attracted any of the deadly Catalina blue sharks. If he were delayed for any reason, he would sometimes be able to retrieve only half a goat.

Just before we left on this trip to Alta in November, Ward had managed to shoot and butcher and freeze seven small, tender goats. It was easy for us to keep the meat he had brought along frozen by keeping it in our sleeping bags in our unheated trailer during the day. At night we took the goat meat out of the sleeping bags and inserted our bodies.

Catalina goat chops are most delicious when fried in a batter of eggs and ground-up saltine crackers. I personally liked to throw a quarter of a handful of sesame seeds into the batter for extra flavor.

What few eggs we had in our trailer were frozen solid and partially covered by shells that shattered during the freezing process. It was no easy trick to lay a frozen egg in a frying pan and thaw it just enough so you could separate the broken shells from the dripping egg at exactly the right time. Then we had to stir the now drippy egg with squashed cracker crumbs and not get too many pieces of eggshell in the mix. We did all this by the light of a kerosene lantern while standing outside in the snow bank behind the trailer with the thermometer hovering between 10 above and 10 below zero.

But one particular Thursday called for something special at dinner.

The sky had been clear all day, and the road up from Salt Lake City had been closed since 8:30 in the morning because of avalanche danger, so we had the mountain almost to ourselves. Our ski technique was bad, and our equipment was worse. Our wooden skis were warped, our edges dull, our boots soft, our bindings not safe, our poles heavy and bamboo, and we could find nothing in our instruction book, Downhill Skiing by Otto Lang, that told us anything about skiing in deep powder snow. Even so, we were already looking for untracked powder snow.

During our lunch break on the Alta Lodge front porch, Ward said, "Look up at High Rustler." There we saw two figures that had climbed almost to the top and were emerging from the trees into the middle of one of the world's most perfect ski slope. It had to be the only two skiers at Alta who were capable of skiing the deep, untracked powder of High Rustler: ski school director Alf Engen and his brother Sverre. They laid down a perfect set of figure eights from top to bottom. We had never seen anything like it.

As they finished their figure eights, we turned our attention to our already open can of sardines and began to lay them out on our frozen slices of bread. After finishing our sardine sandwiches, we each ate a pair of peanut butter and jelly sandwiches. At that moment two young ladies sat down next to us. They were from East Hartford, New Hampshire, a long four-day train ride to Salt Lake City. The parents of these two young ladies owned a ropetow resort in that part of the world, which probably meant they could ski a lot better than we could, except for one thing: They had never skied snow deep enough to come up over the tops of their skis.

Agnes was five-foot eleven and probably weighed a trim 120 pounds. Her sister and traveling companion, Abigail, was almost a foot shorter and outweighed her by about 30 pounds. After lunch we skied the rest of the afternoon with them. Both of them could really turn a pair of skis. At one point, while we were standing in the liftline, they found out we were living in the parking lot. Agnes said, "That's just so Western. We just have to see your house on wheels."

So when the lift finally shut down for the afternoon, the four of us trudged up the hill to the Alta Lodge and sat in the lobby for awhile to get warm. Our view out the window allowed Ward and me to analyze the perfect tracks left by the Engen brothers. Then I pointed out the alpenglow on the mountains, the colors changing from white to shades of pink, then red, then purple, and finally different shades of gray. At that inappropriate moment the manager came over and started talking to the ladies about joining him for dinner. We already considered them our dates for the evening, but since we were freeloading on the heat in his lobby we couldn't say much. So we just waited for them to say no. When they did, we silently hoped they had on enough long underwear to stay alive while we cooked their dinner in our outdoor kitchen in the parking lot.

The four of us got up and chatted briefly with Alf and Sverre, who were trolling the lobby for private powder lessons the next day. Then the ladies picked up their after-ski boots, an extra parka each, and we began the long climb through the wooden tunnel that covered the stairs to the parking lot. There sat the Buick convertible and the eight-foot trailer under a foot-and-a-half of snow.

Ward opened up the portable roof to the kitchen and rigged the canvas walls for whatever warmth they might trap from the kerosene lantern and the Coleman stove. Soon the stove was hissing and the lantern cast its flickering light on the deep snow banks that surrounded us. The four of us huddled around the lantern and stove and talked of powder snow, goat meat dinners, rabbit stew, and other things

Western. As we watched the stew pot boil, it became apparent that it needed something added in order to feed four people. So we just threw in another few handfuls of rice and three frozen carrots.

In the soft, flickering light of the lantern, Agnes said, "We have to go down to Salt Lake City on the bus at seven o'clock, and if we stay for dinner someone will have to drive us down. What if we buy you a tank of gas, and you can drop us later at our hotel? Besides, we have never eaten goat-meat chops."

"It's a deal," we said.

Ward and I had learned early in our winter travels to cook a meal, eat it quickly, throw the dishes in our rucksack and get to the nearest lodge before we froze to death. As a result we had never invested in chairs or a table of any kind. Instead we just stood around stamping our feet as we ate.

By now Agnes and Abigail were stealing what-have-we-gotten-ourselves-into glances at each other. When we went through our thawing-out-the-frozen-egg routine, their expression turned to fear. After mixing the thawed eggs with frozen, squashed crackers, I set about preparing two of our remaining goat-meat chops. They were frozen together so tightly it took a hammer and a screwdriver to pry them apart. Goat-meat chops were our specialty, and I really wanted the ladies to have this special treat. But when your hands are as cold as mine were, it's hard to direct the path of a ballpeen hammer against the top of a screwdriver in the dark. Besides that, my work surface, four inches of ice over an asphalt parking lot, was fairly slippery. I held the frozen chops on edge between my knees and after six or eight whacks with the hammer against the screwdriver, they finally became two separate and distinct chops ready for the frying pan.

The fried goat-meat chops and the hamburger and rice stew finished cooking at about the same time, but now we had another problem: We had only two cups, two plates, two knives, two forks and two spoons. We let the ladies eat the goat-meat chops using the knives, forks and plates, while we spooned down some hamburger and rice stew from our tin cups.

When they finished their goat meat and we finished our cup of Thursday stew, we traded plates, cups and eating utensils after rinsing them in the powder snow just outside the canvas walls of our kitchen. The next course went down as fast as the temperature was dropping, and now it was time for a scalding hot cup of tea with a lot of sugar to ward off the chill. The ladies were really beginning to stomp their freezing feet, so it was no surprise when they offered to buy tea for us in the lodge. Why not? We could do our dishes in the men's room at the same time.

Pots and pans and eating utensils were quickly dumped in the dishwashing rucksack. Ward put out the lantern, closed up the roof to the kitchen, and we started back across the now moonlit parking lot towards the Alta Lodge's tunnel of stairs. At the bottom of the 214 stairs, Ward excused himself and said he would do the dishes and then go back and try to get the car started for the trip down to Salt Lake. "If I do that," he said, "the heater might be working by the time we are all ready to leave."

Half an hour later I was almost asleep in front of the fireplace when Ward returned and announced, "The car won't start. The battery is frozen."

With apologies to the ladies, we were able to locate an empty room in the lodge that they could rent for the night—two rollaways in the kitchen, but at least it was warm.

As the waning full moon came up over the mountains to the east and 10 million stars pierced the blackness of the night, we went back to the trailer, put away our clean dishes, and started to get ready for another great night's sleep wrapped in our mummy bags in our eight-foot trailer in the Alta parking lot.

Before we nodded off, I congratulated Ward on his story about the frozen battery. Then we each had a frozen fig bar from our hidden stash above the bed and went to sleep.

Leftover Chicken Legs

I n the summer of 1947, needing a little more going-skiing money for the upcoming winter, I parted with my old handmade trailer for $150, sold my three-speed bicycle and my high school letter-man's sweater, my Boy Scout uniform and my slightly worn, high-top, black-kangaroo-leather Sam Barry basketball shoes. I put that money together with my wages from digging ditches, hitched my brand-new demo trailer to my beat-up high-mileage 1946 Ford business coupe and was ready to go skiing with my friend and partner Ward Baker for another winter.

On top of the trailer I lashed half-a-dozen pairs of old but freshly varnished skis with genuine metal edges. Then Ward arrived with his collection of skis and assorted paraphernalia, and we started off on our second season-long ski trip.

First stop: Yosemite National Park. We arrived just after Christmas and found the valley packed. But lucky for us there was six inches of snow on the valley floor, and the public campground where we parked the trailer was completely empty. Not surprisingly we were the only campers in Yosemite at that time of year.

Unfortunately, our meager budget didn't include money for food or lift tickets.

On December 27 we found a benefactor for our stomachs, a young busboy at the Badger Pass base lodge named Bob Maynard. (In later years Bob would become president of Keystone, Colorado; Sundance, Utah; and finally Aspen, Colorado.) Since it was a 20-mile trip from the valley to the skiing at Badger Pass, the Awahnee Hotel supplied all of its skiing guests with a fabulous box lunch to take along. Bob collected leftover chicken legs from the deluxe Awahnee box lunches for us. He

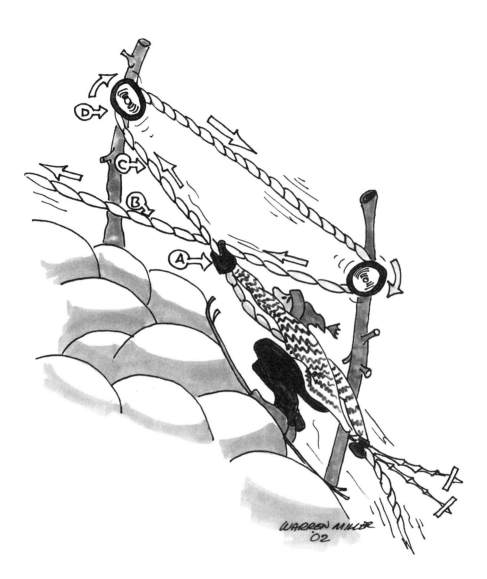

also gathered all of the debris from the lunch tables, extra sandwiches, the occasional pear, apple or banana and even once in a while a leftover carton of milk or a hard-boiled egg. He had a special Warren Miller-Ward Baker depository of day-old food right alongside the garbage cans behind the lodge. What we didn't eat right away we could save. It didn't even have to be put in the icebox, because our whole trailer was an icebox, just as cold inside as outside.

With what turned out to be considerable foresight, I had saved my Yosemite ropetow tickets as souvenirs from the winter before. The second thing I would do every morning after driving up to Badger Pass was go over to the ticket window and check out what color ropetow tickets they were selling that day. Going back to our trailer, I would then carefully select one of seven different colors from my complete collection of lift tickets. Next I would very carefully staple the chosen ticket of the day to my Army surplus parka and then go over and ride the two-dollar-a-day ropetow all day for free.

The Badger Pass ropetow was fantastic. There has never been another one like it anywhere in the world.

The lower half of the hill was very steep, but halfway up it flattened out quite a bit. To keep the rapidly moving rope from digging into the ridge where the slope flattened out, the rope continued on up into the air past where the hill flattened until it was about 15 feet above the snow. There it went around a sheave wheel, reversing its direction and continuing back down the hill for 50 feet or so to another sheave wheel, where it once again reversed direction and started back up the hill, this time at a much flatter angle.

To successfully ride to the top of this unusual ropetow you had to let go of the lower rope, coast the last 10 feet up the steep hill, then grab the upper rope with your remaining strength while hurtling along at 15 miles an hour.

If you could figure out how to do it.

At the bottom, when you squeezed your hands hard enough around the lower rope to start your skis moving uphill, you would squeeze a gallon or more of freezing cold water out of the soggy rope as it went racing through your expensive gloves. As it poured out, it sprayed wet hemp droppings all over your just-back-from-the-dry-cleaner ski clothes.

Today, a lot of ropetow riders would probably be smoking that hemp instead.

On cold days the 15-mile-an-hour rope would be frozen like a long, fast moving icicle. Then it would burn the palms of your leather gloves as you tried to get enough friction with your frozen fingers to start your sticky skis moving.

About every half hour, some first-time ropetow rider would let go of the steep rope and reach for the flat rope. Instead, the skier would re-grab the same steep rope and be hauled 15 or 20 feet up in the air before he or she would:

1) Let go of the rope and fall to the ground in an embarrassed heap.

2) Scream loud enough for the lift operator at the bottom to hear so he could shut off the ropetow, hopefully before the frightened, confused airborne skier would be sucked through the top sheave 20 feet above the snow.

3) Let go of the rope and fall to the ground, whereupon the people clinging to the rope behind would have to steer their skis off to the side of the ropetow track so they wouldn't impale him with their ski tips.

4) Let go of the steep rope too soon and slide backward into the four or five other people who were still riding up the steep part of the hill. The whole group would then slide, roll and tumble to the bottom with their bodies all mixed together like a goal line stand by the Denver Broncos. The frantic screaming of the group was always a signal for the ropetow operator to quit hustling a snow bunny, slowly get up from his chair in the sun and reach for the switch to turn off the ropetow motor. Then it would take a couple of minutes for the sliders to untangle themselves one by one.

One particular goal line pile-up involved a lady whose rental ski boots where way too big. She eventually wandered in a daze back to the lodge in her stocking feet, all the while blaming her ski instructor for not teaching here how to lace her rented ski boots tight enough.

Charlie Proctor was the manager of Badger Pass at the time. He had been on the 1928 Olympic team, and he was also the first person to ever ski down the Headwall at Tuckerman Ravine in New Hampshire.

He offered Ward and me jobs shoveling moguls for 25 cents an hour. Why not? We could earn as much as two dollars a day. Eight hour of shoveling would translate to 10 gallons of gas.

After that first day of shoveling, we rounded up our leftover chicken legs from Bob Maynard and were talking to Charlie near the garbage cans behind the Badger Pass cafeteria. We told him we were eventually going to go on to Sun Valley and pursue the life of a downhill ski racer. He wished us luck but told us, "If you continue to work on the ski patrol shoveling snow, you will become professional skiers and won't be allowed to race. The Olympic amateur rules clearly state that any athlete who has an unfair advantage over another athlete by engaging in monetary remuneration in the pursuit of their chosen sport is automatically a professional."

I was shocked. My dream of a career as a ski racer looked to be in immediate jeopardy. So Ward and I quit right on the spot. I hated shoveling bumps anyway.

From Yosemite to Sun Valley in those days you traveled over 7,227-foot Donner Summit on a two-lane road. We tucked in behind an 18-wheeler that was struggling up the steep Sierra in double compound low gear—and we could still barely keep up with him! Before long a line of about 130 cars was strung out behind us, every driver blaming the trucker for the six-mile-and-hour ascent.

Since we had never skied at Nevada's only resort, Sky Tavern, on the side of Mt. Rose, about 20 miles from Reno, we decided to stop there first. Going down the east side of Donner Summit, Ward and I stopped and cooked up some roadkill that was probably a little too flat. It turned out to be a little too old, too. As a result, we both spent the next three days in bed while camped in the Sky Tavern parking lot, too sick to get out of bed and too sick to stay in it. Every other minute or so we thought we were going to die; in the minutes in between we wished that we would. We should have parked closer to the bathrooms.

When we finally left for Sun Valley four days later, we had still never skied Nevada's only ski resort.

This was the first winter we could afford genuine anti-freeze in the radiator of our car. No more sleeping behind gas stations at night after draining our radiator. We could now sleep anywhere we felt that the sheriff wouldn't wake us up in the middle of the night and run us off. What seemed to work best for us was sleeping behind all-night restaurants. While one of us would talk with the night shift waitress, the other would use the men's room to brush his teeth and shave. We even took a sponge bath occasionally—if we found enough paper towels.

Moving the car in the morning after sleeping behind a truck stop was always hard, because the grease in the bearings would be frozen rock hard. As a result, the trailer wheels refused to revolve for the first 100 yards or so until we drove off of the ice and onto the asphalt highway.

One morning when the trailer wheels slid off the ice and hit the asphalt, the car bumper and the trailer parted company. We drove off leaving most of our worldly possessions behind. We hardly noticed the lurch of the car as the trailer separated from it, because our car always lurched along the first few miles every morning anyway.

About 10 minutes down the road, the rear window of the car unfogged enough for Ward to notice that we weren't being followed by our bedroom and kitchen on wheels. When we finally got back to the truck stop, we found that our trailer had skidded up against the side of an 18-wheel sheep truck. The impact had knocked open one of the truck's tailgates and 137 sheep had walked across the roof of the trailer and were now being rounded up by the Basque truck driver. He could talk to the sheep but couldn't understand a single word we were hollering at him.

An hour later the sheep were finally rounded up and loaded back into the truck. We had mucked the sheep manure off the roof of our trailer and were once again hitched up and heading for Wells, Nevada, where we would turn north to our winter vacation spot, the Sun Valley parking lot.

In the snow-covered hay fields just north of Shoshone, where we had had such good luck shooting rabbits the year before, we parked alongside the road and launched our first rabbit safari of the winter. Ward again brought along his ancient .410-gauge shotgun and his even older single-shot .22-caliber rifle. We already had one year's experience under our belts as white hunters, so it only took about an hour to nail an even dozen rabbits.

We would scare a rabbit up and, while it was running for cover, I would fire a .410 shotgun blast at it. If I missed, which I did about half the time, Ward would whistle loud enough to be heard a mile away. With its big sensitive ears ringing, the rabbit would halt in its tracks. Ward would then kneel down, take careful aim and hit one almost every time.

At about dusk we arrived in Sun Valley and backed our new trailer into the same spot under the same aspen tree where we had parked the year before. I knew it was the same spot because a milk carton, now faded from a year in the sun, was still hanging from a tree branch about 30 feet overhead. The previous winter we had buried our garbage behind the trailer in the snowbank. Then a rotary snowplow had come through the parking lot and thrown our buried garbage all over the trees. I had retrieved most of it, but apparently not all of it.

After unhitching the trailer and parking the car alongside, we headed for the showers at the Skiers Chalet. We knew the Sun Valley system very well, and that free hot shower felt good after our 300-mile trip across the wilds of Nevada and Idaho.

Now squeaky clean with our hair slicked down with Brylcreme, (I had hair in 1947) we roamed the lobbies of the Inn, the Lodge, the drugstore and the bowling alley to see who was still there from the previous season. Sure enough, we met some of our old friends and were introduced to some new ones. Like Betty Bell, who was working the soda fountain in the drugstore. She made us the biggest, thickest and best pineapple milkshake east of Burbank. And for an incomparable price: 30 cents.

Then we sized up the employees at the Inn sports desk. They were the ones who sold lift tickets. Without a pipeline to them, we would have to climb up past the River Run lift every morning to the bottom of the Canyon lift, where no one ever checked your ticket. Our other options were: Pay the $4 a day for a ticket or $200 for a season pass. We didn't have either amount.

At about midnight, the unthinkable happened. We woke to the sound of rain pounding on the trailer roof. Next morning we found out it had rained all the way up to the Roundhouse restaurant at the 8,000-foot level on Baldy. The tropical rainstorm lasted two very long days and then the skies cleared and there wasn't a cloud in the Idaho sky for the next 32 days. During that time the thermometer never rose above zero degrees Fahrenheit and dropped as low as 38 below zero for three days straight. From the bottom of River Run to the top of Canyon, you needed ice skates instead of skis. This was before the invention of offset edges, metal skis or any knowledge of the benefits of torsional rigidity in a ski. For 32 days you could only ski from the top of Baldy down to the Roundhouse. At the end of the day, everyone on the mountain had to ride down the Canyon and River Run lifts—all the instructors, all the pupils, the ski school director, Otto Lang, and every member of the ski patrol.

For the first time in the 11-year history of Sun Valley, the chairlift at the top of Baldy ran all day long without an empty chair.

The Parking Lot
Ski Team

I n January 1948, after an unexpected tropical rainstorm followed by a precipitous drop in the temperature, the bottom two-thirds of Sun Valley's Bald Mountain solidified into dark blue ice. So Ward Baker and I spent a lot of our time practicing slalom on a south-facing slope in front the Roundhouse restaurant. There was no ski lift there, so every time we made a practice run through the gates we had to climb back up. Even though the temperature was always around zero, the constant climbing back up after every run made us sweat so much we stripped down to our T-shirts. We used two-inch aspen trees for slalom poles, and, especially with a T-shirt on, those aspen trees would scuff up your body when you hit them.

Late in January, after running a lot of slalom, I heard from the ski patrol that there was to be a giant slalom the next weekend at Bogus Basin ski area near Boise. Ward and I talked it over and decided this would be our very first official ski race.

The Sun Valley Ski Club already had a hot racing team going to the race. Since both Ward and myself were entrepreneurial (some called us cheap), we asked the ski club to buy our gasoline for our trip to Boise for the race. We would, after all, be representing the club, and we considered it only fair that the club should subsidize us.

"Why should we give you any money?" the club secretary demanded. "We already have our team, and besides, you're only Class C racers." (She had never seen us ski, but she had seen where we lived.)

We left for Bogus Basin early so we could get a good camping spot close to the base lodge, the ropetow, the T-bar and the toilet. The narrow two-lane road up to Bogus had about a thousand switchbacks, and a few miles out of Boise the asphalt stopped and the mud began. By the

Standouts in Eccles Cup

Suzanne Harris of Salt Lake City, left, and Warren A. Miller of Yosemite, Calif., won the feature events of the Eccles cup for men and women at Snow basin Sunday. Miss Harris paced the ladies' field and Miller was the best performer among the men.

From The Salt Lake Tribune Jan. 28, 1948.

time we got to the freezing level, we had 500 pounds of Idaho mud stuck to the bottoms of our car and trailer. Then the muddy ruts gradually turned to frozen, axle-deep trenches from which there was no escape. Despite all that, we made it.

Parking the Ford and the trailer close to the base lodge, we got our ski gear together, registered for the race, picked up our free lift tickets and our racing bibs and headed for the T-bar.

In both my seasons of skiing, I had never even seen a T-bar, much less ridden one. I skied over to the lift with an air of nonchalance, flashed my free lift ticket and the racing bib that was tied around my waist the way the hotshots did it. The lift operator handed me a heavy wooden T-bar hanging from a steel cable that was almost dragging on the ground. I put it behind my knees where I thought it belonged, and when the steel cable unwound to the end of its spring, the wooden T-bar lurched forward and I fell over backward with all the dignity of a real klutz.

Despite the fact that rocks and stumps were sticking out everywhere, the Bogus Basin Ski Club had set a good course. For gates they had used pine two-by-two's that looked like fence posts. Grooming machinery had not yet been invented in 1948, so race courses were a lot bumpier, a lot slower and required a lot more turns than they do today.

The Sun Valley Ski Team looked hot. Each member was wearing a different yet very expensive uniform, including what everyone called in those days a lost-and-found parka ("You lost it, I found it"). Ward and I felt like poor relatives from down in the hollow. I had on my $3 baggy Army surplus pants, my $17 Chippewa ski boots, and my $19 Northland racing skis with genuine Dover toe irons. But I had a million dollars worth of determination.

The giant slalom went off very nicely, with only three racers falling and no one getting injured. Ward and I had to start way at the end of the pack, because we were only C racers with no racing record whatsoever. But because of the icy course, we didn't have to worry about ruts building up.

After the race was over, the officials and all of the gatekeepers got together and tallied up the results. Stan Tomlinson from Boise won, and for some reason I was right behind him, finishing second. Ward place fifth. There was obvious disappointment among the official Sun Valley Ski Club team when they realized that the Parking Lot Ski Team had beaten them handily.

Late Sunday afternoon we started down the long, frozen, rutted two-lane road with its thousand switchbacks. Within a few miles, about a dozen cars were lined up behind us, their drivers impatiently wanting to get by. Suddenly a car behind me made a sharp left turn and disappeared off the road, over the side of the hill. I thought he had blown a tire and that we would find all the occupants dead. I stopped, got out and looked over the edge, only to discover that the car had taken a well-rutted shortcut between the switchbacks. By the time we had rounded a few more curves, all the cars that used to be behind us were now ahead of us. We were tempted to try the next available shortcut ourselves, but Ward wisely decided we might spill all the dishes in the trailer.

Practicing slalom the next day in Sun Valley on the slope near the Roundhouse, there was a lot of good-natured kidding about "the Miller Method of Missing Gates" and not getting caught. It was a little embarrassing to have beaten the entire Sun Valley Ski Club team when I was only a C racer, but not too embarrassing. I still have that Paul Brooks Memorial Giant Slalom Trophy somewhere in my garage along with a few other trophies collected over the years. I think they are in a box between the chainsaw and the wheelbarrow with the flat tire, right under the chair I'm going to fix someday.

Already looming on the ski racing schedule for the next weekend was a giant slalom at Snowbasin near Ogden, Utah. Unfortunately, Ward contracted the flu and decided to take the bus back to Manhattan Beach to recover. Neither of us realized it would take him almost a month to get well and that he wouldn't be able to represent the Parking Lot Ski Team at the second big race of the season.

We had been practicing slalom with Dean Perkins from Ogden and Don McDonald from Seattle. Don had spent the summer skiing in South America with three-time world champion Emile Allais. He returned to Sun Valley speaking just enough French and Spanish to charm half the single ladies in town, as well as the married ones.

Don used all the hot ski gear that went with the French Technique. He wore eight-foot longthongs (leather straps) designed to hold your heel down and give your soft leather ski boots a little more ankle support. He also skied with the radical new ruade technique favored by Emile Allais. (Don't ask me to explain it. That would take a hundred pages of six-point type.)

Neither Don, Dean nor I were allowed to be members of the Sun Valley Ski Club team, so we had to figure another way to get to Ogden. We decided that I would furnish my car, Don would buy gas, and Dean would furnish his mother's basement in Ogden.

Today the trip from Sun Valley to Ogden is mostly an easy five-hour drive on an almost straight four-lane freeway. Then it was a 10-hour drive, for a variety of reasons, some of which are listed here:

1) The road was two-lane, icy and winding all the way.

2) We didn't leave Sun Valley until after we had finished tuning up our racing skills on Friday and until Don had gotten off from his job washing dishes in the Lodge. It was about five o'clock when we left, and what snow had melted on the road was once again turning to ice.

3) The tires on my car were as slick as a bowling ball, so we couldn't go over 30 miles an hour without doing the occasional 360-degree spin. After three of these, plus a 720, I slowed to 25 miles an hour for the rest of the trip.

4) We stopped twice to examine roadkill deer. We wanted to see if it was fresh enough to take to Dean's house for the scheduled Saturday night potluck dinner with his parents.

5) I was still young and hadn't yet learned to read a gas gauge, so we ran out of gas in the middle of the night in the middle of nowhere.

We coasted to a stop about a mile and a half from a farm. My common sense told me that the farmer probably had a tractor somewhere near the barn. After losing a coin flip, I started down the road in search of a couple of gallons of gas while Don and Dean crawled into the back of the car to go to sleep.

We were lucky: The farmer had parked his tractor right near the highway. Still, it wasn't easy to drain out two gallons of gas without alerting the farmer's dogs. I accomplished the job by using the sneaky skills I had learned in amphibious training while in the Navy. (My military career was finally good for something.) Then I trudged a mile and a half back up the icy, windblown road with a gallon can of gas in each hand.

With frozen hands I overdid the priming, and what gas didn't get into the carburetor spilled over onto the engine. Then, while I held the choke wide open, Dean hit the starter. The explosion and small fire caused by the spilled gasoline burned all the fur off the right side of the hood of my Army surplus parka and took some paint off the hood of the car as well.

But the engine coughed to life just as it was advertised to do when you have gas in the tank. I then suggested the following scenario: "Since that tractor is right by the highway, why don't we coast up to it with our engine and headlights turned off? We can siphon out another 10 gallons of gas and leave $3 on the tractor seat with a note and a 50-cent tip. The farmer can easily drive his tractor back to the barn and fill it up again, and we'll have enough gas to get all the way to Ogden."

Fortunately, Donny McDonald had $3, so the deed was done, *almost* without a hitch. We were siphoning the last couple of gallons of tractor gas into the Ford when Dean accidently hit the horn. Instantly half a dozen dogs started barking and running our way, and a moment later lights went on in the farmhouse. I jumped in the car and managed to get it moving before any of the attack dogs had time to bite a hole in a tire.

Fifteen minutes later I began to fall asleep, so I turned the driving chores over to Dean and crawled in the back. A short three hours later I got up and staggered into Dean's mother's basement for what was left of another good night's sleep in the life of a downhill ski racer.

The next morning, in the lodge at Snowbasin, we met up with our pals from the Sun Valley Ski Club team. We picked up our racing bibs, our free lift tickets for the day and our chits for a free lunch. The base lodge was very crowded because the race was being held during semester break, and a half-dozen college ski teams were there, from schools such as U.C.L.A., Stanford and the University of Utah. There was a grand total of 110 competitors in all the various categories, A, B and C.

With a late start number because of my C classification, I had time to get ready for the race like the hotshots did. I sidestepped back up the course for one last look before my number was called, and I watched the top-seeded racers go by one by one, making mental notes as to where they were making mistakes and where the course was rutted.

And then it was my turn.

"Five, four, three, two, one, go!"

And go I did. The snow was soft but well packed with no ice. My $19 skis worked great, and it seemed I had even picked the right wax.

At 3:30 I was sitting around the warming hut comparing skiing experiences with the other racers when the officials announced the third-place winner, the second-place winner and finally the first-place winner: "The winner of the Eccles Cup Giant Slalom, racing for the Sun Valley Parking Lot Team, is...WARREN MILLER!"

I had beaten 109 racers. Of course, I was still only a C racer, but at least now I was earning the points to eventually become a B racer.

Moguls and Michelangelo

When you have no money, buying a lift ticket is a big problem. During the first winter that Ward Baker and I lived in ski resort parking lots all over the West, we solved our lift-ticket problem dozens of different ways, most of them on the fine edge of propriety. How we managed to get so many lift tickets fastened to our parkas without spending any money, or getting caught doing it, will go to our graves with us.

The second winter we lived in the Sun Valley parking lot, however, I acquired my season ski pass in a very unique, yet very honest and hard-working way. I created a job working part time for Sun Valley's manager, Pat "Pappy" Rogers, a job that would allow me to ski every day.

About a week after we set up camp in the parking lot, I went to Pappy's office with the following idea: I would paint cartoon ski scene murals on the walls of the Skier's Dining Room. I told him I would be glad to trade painting the murals for a season pass worth $200. Pappy liked the idea but said he needed to talk to Sun Valley's resident artist, Max Barsis, to see if Max wanted to paint them. Max had been around Sun Valley since the resort opened in 1936.

"You understand, don't you, Warren?"

Quite honestly, I didn't.

Pappy Rogers was a much more understanding human being than I was. He was also the best manager of any ski resort in the world then and would probably be the best even today. Two days later, Pappy stopped by our trailer one morning and woke me up with a cup of coffee. He said, "Warren, Max wants to paint your murals. Off the record, though, he just didn't want you, the parking lot artist, to paint them. But since it was your idea, why don't you paint some of your cartoon

They started calling Warren, "The poorman's Michelangelo of the mountains".

murals on the walls of the employees' cafeteria? I'll still give you your season pass. And, by the way, why don't you just eat all of your meals in the cafeteria while you're painting them?"

Within a week all of the guests thought I was an employee, and most of the employees thought I was a guest.

I quickly became the world's slowest mural designer and painter. Those cartoon murals I painted on the walls of a Quonset hut left over from World War II took me longer to paint than Michelangelo took to paint the ceiling of the Sistine Chapel.

Before I started painting the murals, I had already developed a rather large yet very small and rather intimate business in the hospital. I was the only supplier of original cartoons painted on the casts of patients who had just broken their legs. I charged $1 a leg.

In those days, when skiers broke a leg skiing, they really broke it. It was called a spiral fracture, which was just what the words describe: The fracture would spiral up and down the lower leg bone and look just like a coiled spring in the X ray.

To repair such a shattered bone, Dr. Moritz would make a long incision in the lower leg so he could get his hands on all the broken pieces. Then he would rearrange them back into some semblance of normalcy and then wrap stainless steel bands around the pieces to keep them in place until they healed. The patient was put to sleep for the surgery using ether, a very smelly gas that always left patients sick to their stomachs for several hours after they woke up.

I figured out very early, as part of my cast painting business development plan, that I should arrive at the hospital at just about dinnertime. Each evening I would make my rounds of the newly injured, trying to strike a deal with one or more patients to paint my cartoons on their casts. I tried to time my artwork so I could get my cartoons roughed out in pencil about the same time that the patient's dinner arrived. The patient, of course, would be very slowly recovering from the effects of ether, sick to his stomach and unable to eat his dinner. If my timing was just right, he would almost always offer his dinner to me. After a couple of weeks of busy cast painting, it got so the nurses would ask me, instead of the patient, what I would like for dinner.

There were some days when the powder snow, or the crud, was very difficult to ski in, and I could count on at least a couple of hospital meals. I would eat one for dinner, and the other one I would put in the waxed paper I kept in my rucksack. That way Ward and I could have a great lunch the next day. It was a welcome change from our steady diet of oyster-crackers-and-ketchup-in-hot-water soup.

My artistic workload was increasing rapidly. Sometimes I had a tough decision to make. Should I paint cartoons on someone's cast and earn a dollar and get a free hospital meal? Or should I spend the evening working on my employee cafeteria cartoon murals to work off some of my season pass obligation and eat an employee dinner? My decision would depend on what they were serving in the cafeteria that night.

Forty-five years later, that Quonset hut was still standing. However, it has become the laundry and dry cleaning headquarters for the Sun Valley company. At last report, a few of my cartoons were still visible on one of the walls out behind the drum dryer, just before you got to the sheet and pillowcase ironer.

I used good paint.

By this time in my life, cartooning had already saved my financial neck many times. The first time was three years earlier in Yosemite, when I was in the Navy and waiting for orders that would send me back to the South Pacific. I was being paid an extra seven dollars a day for room and board, and I was skiing every day like it was my last. I was also going out somewhere to a party every night knowing that it could be my last night in Yosemite.

When the lifts closed for the day, I would sit in the Badger Pass Lodge and make cartoon sketches of funny things that happened while skiing with my friends that day. I'd hang a new one up on the bulletin board each day, and one day someone asked me if he could buy the cartoon I had drawn of them.

"Sure, I'll sell it to you for a dollar."

Two cartoons would pay for a one-day ropetow ticket.

Fourteen cartoons later, my earnings bought a different colored lift ticket for every day of the week. From then on I was home free.

Later I put together a collection of those early cartoons in what became my first ski publication, a book I called *Nice Try, George*. I printed 2,000 copies of that book for 50 cents each and sold them for $2 each. (I used the War Bond money I had saved while overseas to pay for the printing.) I also sold the books for $1 each to any ski shop or store that bought a dozen. If they only bought six, I would charge them a $1.25. In Pocatello, Idaho, late one afternoon, I was able to trade a half-dozen books for enough Kraft Dinner to last Ward and me two weeks.

I was very surprised the first time someone in Sun Valley asked me to autograph a copy of my book. What surprised me the most was that the person came out to our trailer early in the morning and woke me up for my autograph. Even more significant was that the person looking for my autograph was the beautiful blonde Norwegian female that I had tried to talk to in the Roundhouse restaurant the day before.

I got dressed in my usual legs-out-of-the-trailer-wrapped-in-sleeping-bag fashion with feathers of all different sizes from my down sleeping bag stuck all over my sweatshirt. Once dressed, I graciously offered her a cup of hot tea. She accepted, so I had to open up the kitchen, pump up the Coleman stove, and melt the ice in the always-ready oatmeal pan.

After our second cup of tea, I made a pot of oatmeal and shared some with her. I was halfway through my bowl of oatmeal when I found out that she was a guest in the Sun Valley Lodge. Anyone staying in the Lodge was G.L.U.E. to me: Geographically Lovely, Undesirable Economically. The cheapest room in the Lodge was $18 a night. That was more than my budget for 108 days of living in Sun Valley. My breakfast guest, Hildegard, helped me clean up the dishes, bought a second autographed book at full retail for her father and invited me to ski with the two of them that day.

Why not?

I met them an hour later at the bus stop by the ski school meeting place and noticed immediately that I was way out of my class. She and her Daddy had the latest, the greatest and the most expensive ski clothes and equipment that money could buy. She wore an Ann Taylor sweater and Jules Andre custom-made $30 gabardine in-the-boot ski pants. They both carried brand new Sigi Engl signature-model plastic-bottomed Northland skis with Luggi Foeger micromatic adjustable toe irons. She also wore a pair of made-to-measure Peter Lemmer boots.

Daddy was a fashion plate in an elegant yet contrasting parka set against a handknit Norwegian sweater with darling handknit mittens to match. He had steel-gray hair and fire in his eyes. It was immediately obvious to me that his daughter had already told him that I was living in "that trailer in the parking lot with a great view of our room in the Lodge." I had already found out that their room was the room in which Ernest Hemingway wrote his famous book *For Whom the Bells Toll*.

I also had a little fire in my eyes and some in my belly, too.

It was usually brought on by hunger.

In spite of all their expensive gear, they both were wearing their handknit white angora socks very conspicuously outside of their ski pants, which gave them away as beginners. Daddy put on his Norwegian accent a little louder so I would assume that this was the way they wore their ski socks in Norway.

Riding the bus to the River Run lift, I felt very out of place. I was sitting alongside Hildegard in my army surplus pants, my sweatshirt, my White Stag windbreaker, and dragging along my really beat-up laminated ridge-top $19 hickory skis. My custom-made in-line Groswold front springs looked hot, though.

Hildegard's Daddy was quiet on the bus ride, but when we got onto the single chairlift he set the tone of the day by belting out a yodel that scared away every elk, deer, squirrel and chipmunk living within a mile and a half. He sounded like a combination tobacco auctioneer and hog caller at the National Western Stock Show.

The chairs on the lift only carried one passenger at a time, so there was no time for intimate, cuddly discussion with Hildegard about her skiing ability or her Daddy's. We would find that out soon enough when we got to the top of Baldy.

I hoped Hilde and her Daddy were good skiers, because there had been a 10-inch snowfall the night before, and I was looking forward to really ripping it up. I always hang back on my first run with new friends, so I can follow along behind and size up their skiing ability. It was a good thing I did this with Hilde and her Daddy, because all 215 pounds of him took off down the hill like an Olympic downhill racer and never looked back...until he caught an edge about a third of the way down the ridge. When the snow cleared, his moans could be heard above his Norwegian swear words. I went to call the ski patrol.

A few minutes later we were standing around waiting for the patrol to arrive, and Hildegard was crying over her Daddy as if her bank account and her ski holiday had cracked up before her very eyes. Her white angora socks that were outside of her ski pants had collected a couple of pounds of new powder snow that was already melting and dribbling down inside her boots. This somewhat obvious phenomenon meant that her feet quickly began to freeze.

Daddy's unfortunate accident drew a ski patrolman who had ingested a large quantity of wine the night before. He was at this precise moment about 80 percent brain dead because of a monumental hangover. We watched him being buffeted by 35-mile-an-hour winds that he created while being chased down a very steep hill by a heavily loaded 150-pound, eight-foot wooden toboggan.

This hungover ski patrolman, with his well-waxed toboggan chasing him, roared right on by the now very large group of skiers who had clustered by the Norwegian Daddy. Probably because of the overabundance of red veins in the patrolman's eyeballs that morning, he never saw any of us. But about a 100 yards below us he finally seemed to realize that he was going about twice as fast as he wanted to.

Defying all the laws of inertia, he made a slight right turn while the toboggan kept going straight. He miraculously got out from in front of it. As he slid to a stop in a cloud of new snow, the toboggan, still loaded with splints, blankets, tarpaulin, medical supplies, wire gurney and all that was left of a half gallon of red wine continued accelerating until it was finally stopped short by a pine tree. Bits and pieces of wooden toboggan, pipe handles, tangled bits of wire gurney, shreds of blankets and a half gallon of red wine blasted into orbit. A few minutes later it all started re-entry and began to slowly but completely cover about an acre and a half of freshly fallen snow.

I heard later that Slingshot Sam the Ski Patrol Man just skied right on down the hill, cleaned out his locker and moved down to Hailey where he got a job as a bag boy at the State Liquor Store.

Meanwhile, back to Hildegard and her formerly yodeling Daddy. A replacement rescue toboggan was being brought down to the scene of the accident by two, more cautious ski patrolmen, one hanging onto a rope behind the toboggan to act as a brake and the other in front to steer it. They slowly sideslipped their way down to the now traumatized group of accident gawkers hovering around the distraught Norwegian.

Every member of the Sun Valley Ski Patrol was qualified to give morphine injections to deaden the pain of a seriously wounded skier, and that's what these two did to Daddy right away. Before long Daddy wasn't screaming and swearing, but he wasn't yodeling either. He was singing *Take the A Train* in Norwegian and asking for another shot of whatever it was the guy in the red parka had already given him.

Thirty minutes later, Hildegard was tearfully sideslipping down alongside her Daddy. He was by then splinted, blanket-wrapped and strapped into the gurney on the toboggan. I had had enough of the whole mess and headed down a south slope, carving turns in the still untracked 10 inches of new powder snow.

That evening I made my usual hospital rounds looking for potential customers for my "Mural on Your Cast" business. In the most expensive private room in the hospital, there was Daddy with his leg in traction. Hildegard was sitting beside the ashen-faced former Norwegian god. When I came into the room with a smile on my face and my cast-mural paint kit in my hand, Daddy took one look at me and exploded, "It was all your fault!"

When I offered to waive my usual $1.50 fee for painting murals on a full-length hip cast, he grabbed what turned out to be a bowl of split pea soup from his dinner tray and threw it in my direction.

I ducked.

When that split pea soup hit the wall, it exploded—and there blended right into the hospital color scheme and went virtually unnoticed by the cleaning staff for almost a week.

Hildegard came out into the hall a few minutes later and apologized for her Daddy's behavior. She then tearfully said, "Daddy forbids me to ever see you again, and if you even try, he'll have the police arrest you for contributing to the accident of the Norwegian consulate to the United States."

Wow. I had just injured my first celebrity.

"I'm sorry for his attitude," I said, "because I sure would like to have seen some of my original art work go back to Washington, D.C., on his cast."

I made one last sales pitch when I told Hilde that for $2 more, many of my customers shipped their casts back to me after they had them taken off. I would make a flower pot out of Daddy's cast for their rumpus room.

I realized that this sales pitch was also going to be unsuccessful when Hilde tearfully replied, "Daddy told me he will cut me off without any money if I ever mention your name again."

They left together on the train to Shoshone as soon as he could travel.

Two Girls, a Frozen Buick and Homemade Ice Cream at Eight Below Zero

Almost due east of the Sun Valley Lodge, a narrow icy road led to a one-lane bridge across Trail Creek just before it emptied into Dollar Lake. In the winter of 1946-47, the road was barely wide enough for two buses to pass and was banked on both sides with snow piled four or five feet high. As it curved slowly to the left and climbed a small hill, it split. The right-hand fork went over to the Dollar Mountain ski lift, while the left-hand fork headed due north to the Ruud Mountain lift, one of five ski lifts that were then operating in Sun Valley. This was the first winter that Ward Baker and I lived in a trailer in the parking lot near the centrally located Sun Valley Lodge, and we could take our choice of almost half of the 12 chairlifts then operating in the world.

Ruud Mountain rose about a 1,000 vertical feet above the road. A small stand of Aspens stood in the center, with a path cut through them for the chairlift. The mountain was too steep for beginning skiers and no longer a challenge to good skiers now that three chairlifts had been built on 9,000-foot Baldy. We rode the Ruud Mountain lift only when we wanted untracked powder snow all to ourselves four or five days after a storm. Free bus service ran to Ruud Mountain, but only when a customer wanted to ski over there. The lift operators at Ruud, who were mostly retired railroad engineers, slept most of the day. One ski patrolman was one more than enough to handle the "crowds." There was no restaurant, no warming hut, no ski school meeting room, just a

Ruud Mountain was the site of the only Nordic ski jumping hill in the state of Idaho.

WARRENISM

"When it comes to skiing, there's a difference between what you think it's going to be like, what's it's really like, and what you tell your friends it was like."

good steep hill for powder snow skiing or for fantastic corn snow skiing in the spring.

But Ruud was also the site of the only Nordic ski jumping hill in the state of Idaho. The ski jump got used only once a year, because interest in Nordic ski jumping was fading rapidly with the proliferation of chairlifts. Called the President's Cup, this early season event combined three ski disciplines: downhill, slalom and Nordic jumping.

Neither Ward nor I had enough experience to race with the good guys, much less jump 180 feet or more. This was our first real season of skiing. However, we knew that the best way to learn how to do these things was to watch the best, and the best skiers from all over the Western United States had gathered in Sun Valley to compete in the President's Cup.

Being creatures of comfort, we were smart enough not to want to sit outside in the bleachers watching ski jumpers perform in eight-degree-below-zero weather. This was long before the invention of the wind-chill factor. Had we known there was such a thing, it would have seemed a lot colder.

Watching from the front seat of our Buick was the logical alternative. And having some female companionship would make it even better. So we talked a couple of waitresses into accompanying us to the jumping.

Unfortunately, our Buick was buried in a snowbank in the parking lot and frozen solid. So we picked a waitress who could borrow a friend's car that was heavy enough to pull our frozen sedan out of the snowbank. Her borrowed car also had to be powerful enough to tow the Buick far enough so I could jump-start it.

When we originally left Southern California, Ward had wisely brought along a manila-hemp mooring line from his tuna fishing boat. It was about 50 feet long, an inch-and-a-half thick and strong enough to keep a tanker tied to a dock.

Our first challenge was trying to get the frozen rope out from under our trailer and uncoiled. Looping the rope around a pair of bumpers and then tying a Boy Scout knot in each end was our next real challenge. It took a blowtorch to accomplish that job.

Ward had packed one of those, too.

Grace eased her borrowed car out ahead of us and slowly straightened out the frozen coils of Ward's mooring-line tow-rope. Unsticking our frozen tires from the ice they had melted into looked like it was going to be a problem, but eventually Grace managed to yank us out and tow us across the parking lot toward the Lodge. However, when I let the clutch out to turn the engine over, the rear wheels simply stopped turning. The engine was frozen solid, and the bald rear tires skidded on the icy surface.

We began to run out of parking lot space. That's when Grace cranked a 15-mile-an-hour hard right turn up the small hill to get onto the road to Ketchum. At that point the rear end of my car gave up any thought of traction and spun almost all the way around to hit Grace's back bumper. She sped up and yanked on the mooring line again, which pulled the front end of my car back in line.

Ward now reappeared from the back seat, where he had sought cover.

Once on the asphalt, my bald tires finally got enough traction to begrudgingly turn the engine over. But each time I popped the clutch the rope pulled taut, and the rear bumper of Grace's borrowed car took on a larger and more ominous semicircular look.

The Buick finally coughed to life, I pumped like crazy on the throttle, and it loped into its old familiar rhythm. Ward waved frantically and I honked the horn continuously to get Grace to slow down. She jammed on her brakes so hard we slammed into her rear bumper. It was no big loss. The crash bent her semicircular bumper back into a reasonable facsimile of its original shape.

Untying the Boy Scout knots in the hemp tow-rope took a long screwdriver, two pairs of pliers, two tire irons, four frozen hands and 20 minutes. But finally we got turned around and drove back to our camping spot in the parking lot. Grace parked her borrowed car as far away from us as she could and made sure to park it with the damaged back bumper buried up against a snowbank.

Then we all jammed into the front seat for warmth and headed for Ruud Mountain.

Arriving at the jump hill, we all agreed that driving had been a wise decision. True, we had bounced off snowbanks a couple of times during the leisurely two-mile trip, but I managed to keep the car out of serious trouble, and we finally slid into an icy parking place alongside the grandstand.

By now the wind had picked up to a steady 15 miles an hour and was gusting to 30. Ward got out a couple of our extra down sleeping bags that still smelled like dead goat meat and old mackerel left over from when we were still storing our original ski vacation provisions in them. The four of us hunkered down in the front seat, sat back, relaxed and tried not to inhale.

High up at the top of the in-run above the jump hill we could see the ski jumpers standing around freezing half to death, waiting their turn to risk death between gusts of wind. In the grandstand, only a handful of people were still huddled together to keep from freezing right where they sat. After half a dozen jumpers flew through the air for a couple of seconds, I could see why most of the people who had come to watch had already gone home. None of the jumpers were falling, and if you've seen one 60-meter jumper jumping 40 meters, you've seen them all.

Now the discussion in the front seat between Ward, Grace, Joan and myself went back and forth. We'd seen enough ski jumping; how would we spend the rest of the afternoon?

1) We could sneak into the Lodge swimming pool.

2) We could go watch bowling.

3) There was still time for a couple of runs if we went back and got our skis and stuff.

That was when Ward came up with one of his great ideas. "Look, I have my ice cream freezer in the trunk of the car, and it's eight below zero out there. I can put in a couple of quarts of milk, some pineapple and all I have to do is stand outside and turn the crank for a little while. We'll have two quarts of homemade pineapple ice cream. We can take it downtown and swap half of it for a couple of hamburgers—and salvage the rest of the afternoon."

I started the engine while Ward put two cartons of frozen milk in a pan and set it on the exhaust manifold that was rapidly heating up.

Ten minutes later the milk was melted enough to pour it into the ice cream freezer.

So while the best skiers in the Western United States were hurtling themselves through the air trying to win the President's Cup, Ward was out at the bottom of the landing hill cranking that ice cream freezer like crazy. The ladies and I cheered him on from the cozy sanctuary of our goat meat- and mackerel-flavored sleeping bags.

When Ward's cranking began to slow down, the three of us in the front seat rolled up the sleeping bags and threw them into the back seat. Ward then put the two quarts of his Ruud Mountain Homemade Pineapple Ice Cream in the back seat, stowed the crank and the bucket in the trunk, and hunkered down in the front seat between the two girls to thaw out his body. We knew the ice cream would keep nicely in the back seat, because it was the same temperature it was outside.

The front seat was the same temperature, too.

Then we drove off to a restaurant in Ketchum where a friend of Grace's worked.

The swap was easily made. Hamburgers with French fries were 25 cents each, so Ward and I sprang for two orders for our dates. We then swapped half of Ward's Ruud Mountain ice cream for a pair of hamburgers and two orders of fries for ourselves. We spent the rest of the afternoon munching on this fabulous 50-cent spread, tucked into a warm restaurant booth and speculating on the following:
1) Would the bent bumper go undetected by the guy who owned our dates' towing car?
2) Who won the President's Cup?

Ward and I congratulated ourselves on being way too smart to take up the soon-to-be-almost-obsolete sport of Nordic ski jumping.

Taking It Straight

Under a clear blue sky, with the temperature hovering around zero, I stood shivering beside the Roundhouse Corner and watched some of America's best skiers race around that left-hand fallaway corner at a frightening rate of speed. The noise from their flapping pants, the hiss of their metal edges against the hard-packed snow and the shouts of the crowd all combined in some psychotic way to make me want to someday be a good enough skier to do the same thing.

"Take the Canyon straight on a pair of skis."

This was the dream of almost everyone we met and skied with in Sun Valley in the late 1940s. If you could take the Canyon straight and survive, you were one of a very elite group of skiers on the mountain. When you consider how bad the equipment was in those days, going that fast was about as safe as bungee jumping without a bungee cord.

Skis were seven-feet, six-inches long and made of very stiff laminated hickory. None of us had ever heard of filing our edges to make them sharper. Beartrap bindings that resembled a partially closed vise held your foot to the ski, no matter which way your leg or your body revolved when you fell.

Nylon parkas hadn't been invented. Mine was poplin, and I always had to wear at least two, and sometimes three, sweaters under it, with long underwear under that to stay warm. There were no thermal long johns then, just good old-fashioned wool long johns, which had a serious design defect. When wool long johns got wet, they would start itching so badly you could hardly sit on the chairlift without squirming. And my long johns got wet a lot, because my $7 gabardine ski pants were anything but waterproof. My here and there hand sewing never

My Chippewa ski boots gave less support than a wet cardboard box of the same thickness.

quite closed up the random rips and tears in them. I had also opted for flaps on my pants pockets, because they were a dollar cheaper than a pair with zippered pockets. I hadn't sewn on buttons to hold the flaps closed, so my pockets were always full of snow. When I went into the warming hut for lunch, the snow in my pockets would melt and get my wool long johns even wetter.

My Chippewa ski boots were made of fairly soft leather that went way up to my ankle bones. They gave even less support than a pair of today's cross-country boots. When they got wet, which happened every day, they gave less support than a wet cardboard box of the same thickness. Their one redeeming value was that they had great big box toes, so my toes never got cold—at least not as cold as the rest of my feet.

Rocketing by our position on the Roundhouse Corner, these men I was watching were trying out for the 1948 Olympic ski team. They were riding the same kind of gear I used and going straight down the Canyon at speeds approaching 50 miles an hour. Two of them had even wrapped shoe laces around their baggy and wildly flapping ski pants to cut down on wind resistance.

I was busy taking pictures of these racers with my eight millimeter, single-lens movie camera so that Ward and I could watch them later and learn how anyone could go so fast and survive.

The racers were taking a flying sideslip to the right through the Rock Garden and then trying to hang onto the snow while they tried to execute that left turn at an unbelievably high speed. A few of them made the turn in a wide snowplow position, ski tips together, heels four feet apart and standing up straight for more wind resistance. They were trying anything short of falling down to slow down. When you combined the poor ski equipment with the very bumpy race courses, the "good old days" were just that—good for the spectator. Ward and I stood there filming, ogling, shivering and wondering if we could ever become good enough skiers to someday ski straight down the Canyon.

Two months later, in early March, on an overcast day while skiing in a snowstorm, I missed a turn near the bottom of the Canyon. Just before going into the Narrows I was suddenly going way too fast to turn. With terror in my heart, I tried to somehow line up on the center of the Narrows where I imagined the bumps converged and would provide a smoother ride. I barely managed to stand up through the Narrows, with my feet wide apart and my arms flailing, while hollering,

"Get out of the way!"

I somehow survived the next two or three hundred yards until I finally got to the bottom of the Exhibition lift in one piece and was getting back on the lift. I realized I had just taken the bottom half of the Canyon straight. It was exhilarating. I wondered how much faster I would be going if I started going straight a little higher up.

Thinking about it, I realized that when I had gotten halfway through the Narrows I had already reached terminal velocity for my size, my very bad ski equipment and my lack of skill: a six-foot, two-inch skinny guy wearing a baggy Army surplus parka and baggy Army surplus pants that flapped violently in the wind. I was also standing up straight with my arms out as far as they would reach for more wind resistance. The wooden bottoms of my scratched-up skis probably slowed me down another 10 or 15 percent. I rationalized that I couldn't go any faster no matter how far up the hill I started; I would just be going at terminal velocity longer.

Halfway up the lift I decided that this was the day I would add my name to the list of people who had taken the Canyon straight.

On the next run, making long turns to relax, I skied about halfway down Canyon and then came to stop on the right-hand side. I stood there for a few minutes and wondered if I could cheat a little bit and line up on the center of the Narrows with a long, slow sideslipping turn and avoid terminal velocity.

I couldn't.

Within 30 yards of where I started, I was going way too fast. Faster than I had ever skied before. Still, I managed to hit the same smooth center line in the Narrows, and as I roared through that part of my speed run, I was out of control big time. But I survived, and as I skied out of the bottom of the Narrows, I even started thinking about pulling my arms in a bit so I could go faster. I was just *thinking* about pulling my arms in; I didn't *actually* pull them in. Going up the lift for the third time, I even thought about putting faster wax on my worn-out

WARRENISM

"Nobody can make you feel inferior without your consent except a ski instructor."

skis, but I let that thought pass, too.

I only wanted to do one thing: I wanted to be able to say to myself, "Starting at Roundhouse Corner, I took the Canyon straight." I was doing it just for the bragging rights, not to set any records.

This time, with another long sideslipping turn, I started my run just below the Roundhouse Corner, almost at the top of the Canyon. Whoosh! I was out the other end of the Narrows at a speed approaching 357 miles an hour. Or so I thought. Approaching 50 miles an hour in my second season on skis was plenty fast enough for me then. And it still is today.

By the time I got to the top of the Exhibition lift the fourth time, word had reached the Roundhouse that I was working my way up to take the Canyon straight. A large crowd of at least three or four of my waitress and kitchen-help friends came out to watch me crash and burn. And two of my ski patrol friends were trying to talk me into letting them wax my skis. They were calling me chicken for not getting into a crouch now that I was starting from the top. One of them had dozens of straight-down-the-Canyon notches in his skis. Some of his no-turn trips he had even done without tightening his boots.

"Miller, you're yellow! Go from the top."

"No snowplowing!"

"Quit sideslipping down and start up where the good guys do."

After a short side trip out into the trees to relieve my nervousness, I decided to go for it. And why not? All that could happen to me was to crash and have my vice-like, never-release beartrap bindings end my ski season if I made a mistake of any kind.

This was before the invention of safety bindings and Blue Cross.

Amid the shouts of the hordes of spectators—there were now five of them—I timidly shoved off and got into the fall line while still in a snowplow. I didn't dare skate for more speed, and in the first 50 yards I was glad I had made that trip into the trees. Danger is a cumulative commodity, and going this fast for such a long time greatly increased my odds of crashing with each bump I hit. At the start of the run, I had momentarily tucked my arms close to my body. By now, however, I was reaching out for any kind of braking effect I could achieve with wind resistance. Somehow I had to slow down.

"Come on, parka and pants: flap more and slow me down," I shouted.

As I plummeted into the Narrows, the back pressure of the wind finally slowed me down to about 40 miles an hour. Now I had only to hang on for another 100 yards, and I would be out on the other side of the Narrows.

I made it. I had finally taken the Canyon straight. I had done it once from top to bottom, and I was still alive. I took stock of my current physical condition:

Arms? Not broken.

Legs? Not broken.

Brain? Not broken.

Hey, I took the Canyon straight.

Do I need to do it again?

Of course not!

And I never did.

The Girl and the DC-3

he was a very pretty, dignified graceful lady, who exuded a lot of animal magnetism. In short, she was a turn on. Not a very good a skier by today's standards, but rather good by 1947 standards. She spent all day every day on Dollar Mountain under the guidance of a $20-a-day private ski instructor, and every one of her ski vacation evenings was spent with me. It might have blossomed into a long-term romance, but our worlds, unfortunately, were very far apart. She was from Texas, and I was from California. She was living in a very expensive room in the Sun Valley Lodge, and I was living in a trailer in the parking lot. Her room was $18 a night, and my camping place was $18 for the winter. That didn't keep the two of us from going bowling in the Lodge basement or walking down to Ketchum for an evening of wandering in and out of all the gambling halls and watching the high rollers play roulette or attending quite a few movies together. I had a secret method of using the same two theater tickets over and over.

I wish I could write that ours was a torrid romance. Not in those days. But we are still good friends today, she after five husbands and me through the death of my first wife and the divorce of my second. In fact, she is one of my wife Laurie's best friends and ski companions.

When it came time for her leave, I told her I would be very happy to give her and her roommate a ride down to the Hailey Airport. Apprehensive that my frozen car wouldn't start, I began preparations for the 12-mile journey to Hailey a couple of hours before their scheduled departure.

To start the car, I used "the-coffee-can-half-full-of-gas" trick. You first puncture holes in the side of a one-pound coffee can about one-third of the way up from the bottom. This will let air in so that the gasoline will burn at the bottom of it. Then you pour gasoline in the can, light it on fire and shove it under the frozen engine of the car. In theory, the flames will be just high enough and burn long enough to warm up the engine and the oil. It will also light your car on fire if you don't know what you are doing. I had started our car this way a couple of dozen times, so I had the equation for the right amount of gasoline versus the air temperature figured out pretty well. As cold as it was, I figured an eight-minute mini-furnace was about the right

I must offer a few words of caution when you use this method to heat up your engine.

1) Be sure to have a long wire connected to the can so you can drag it out from under the car if the flames get big enough to scare you.

2) Have a long stick at the ready so you can move the flaming can of gasoline around while it is under the car.

3) MOST IMPORTANT. Have the hood open and a big shovel ready so you can throw a lot of snow on the engine if the fire gets out of control.

By the time I picked Josephine and Audrey up in front of the Lodge, I smelled like I had just put out a fire in an oil refinery. I let Max the bell captain figure out how to get their 11 suitcases stacked in the trunk, the back seat and tied onto the front fenders of the car. He had to take out the ice cream freezer, the mackerel-smelling sleeping bag and the duffel bag with two weeks of dirty clothes to get them all in. I made sure he put my stuff in a place where no one would think it was trash and throw it out while I was driving the ladies to the airport.

Driving to Hailey we must have looked like a family of Texas sharecroppers headed for California during the great Depression. Upon closer examination, however, the ladies' expensive pigskin luggage gave away our secret.

We skidded through the left turn in Ketchum and started south toward Hailey. Just out of town, dropping down to cross the bridge over Trail Creek, we climbed slowly up the other side, and the ladies

took one last look at the skiers on Baldy. Then we made the slow curve to the left by Smith Farnum's barn, his house and his feedlot, where I would one day shoot a lot of rabbits on full-moon nights. The three of us talked about skiing together again someday, sometime, some place.

I managed to get them safely to Hailey and to the airport without skidding off the road.

What an airport!

It was a plowed grass field that had been rolled flat by a steam roller when the owner/operator had a couple of days off from working on the highway. There were a couple of hangers, no control tower. There was, however, a little gravel here and there on what slightly resembled an airport runway. Standing out there all by itself was a ramp with two wheels, four or five steps and a piece of plywood attached to the side with bailing wire. Painted on the side was a sign that said, "Welcome to Hailey, Idaho, Gateway to Sun Valley." This ramp apparently was available for the occasional two-engine airplane that might show up from Hollywood. Alongside of it was a four-by-four post with a box nailed to it. In that box was a fire extinguisher and a small first aid kit. I looked in the kit, and there were only a few Band-

Aids and some iodine. Someone must have felt that this would be sufficient in the event of a crash landing. Oh, yes: There was also a telephone number for who to call in an emergency. However, there was no phone to use.

We sat there together and waited for their plane to arrive. There wasn't another car to be seen anywhere, except for the occasional one that would drive by on the way south toward Shoshone. I had assumed Josephine and Audrey would fly out on some sort of a commercial plane, but didn't think too much about it at the time. Finally, I heard the engines of a plane approaching from the south.

As it got closer, I was reminded of a scene out of the old movie *Lost Horizon* with Ronald Coleman, the sun flashing off a very small, almost invisible speck in the sky with the ancient rounded snow-covered hills to the southeast forming a backdrop that only a movie director could have dreamed up. As it slowly got closer, I was finally able to tell that it was a DC-3 but couldn't make out any commercial markings on it. Even after the pilot eased it onto the ice- and snow-covered runway, raising a giant cloud of blowing snow, then turned it around and taxied back to our car, it was still impossible to read any markings on it.

While the pilot was still taxiing, I got out and started to unload all the suitcases. I began to wonder if the plane would be big enough to fly the two of them and all their luggage clear back to Texas.

Then the rear cabin door swung down, and the pilot and co-pilot climbed out. The pilot brought greetings from Josephine's father, who, it seemed, owned the plane.

Now it really became a scene out of a movie. He unloaded a table and four chairs, three picnic baskets full of food and a couple of bottles of wine, crystal glasses and sterling silver place settings. While all of this was going on, I was schlepping the suitcases out of my derelict 1937 Buick.

Finally, I took a tentative look inside the plane. The interior was like nothing I had ever seen in my life: It contained leather seats, plush carpeting and what looked like gold-plated ash trays. I was assured, however, that they were not really gold plated.

"I asked our pilot to bring plenty of food with him from Texas, because I didn't think I could get a caterer to restock our plane in Hailey, Idaho," Josephine explained.

The luggage easily fit into what turned out to be a cavernous luggage compartment and then we sat there warm and toasty in the reflection of the shiny aluminum side of the aircraft, eating roast beef sandwiches, seafood cocktails, a great Caesar salad and a chocolate cake that anyone would die for.

Finally, what was left of the food was put back in the picnic baskets and the plane was made ready for takeoff. Hugs and kisses all around. Addresses and phone numbers exchanged. Then the pilot took me aside and told me where to stand and what to do with the fire extinguisher when he started up his engines.

As the second engine fired up and the pilot saluted just like John Wayne used to, I backed out of the way with the fire extinguisher at the ready, and he began taxiing to the west end of the runway. Josephine and Audrey waved good-bye and blew kisses from the miniature windows. At the far end of the runway the pilot set his brakes, revved up the engines and checked his ailerons, his horizontal and vertical stabilizer and, with his engines at almost full throttle, he released the brakes and started lumbering down the bumpy runway with a giant plume of wind-driven snow curling up behind him. Then the plane lifted off and headed for Texas in that dark blue winter sky.

Renegade Instructor

In December 1948, at the start of my third winter in Sun Valley, I heard that tryouts for new ski instructors were taking place over on Dollar Mountain. The Sun Valley Ski School was going to pay $4 a day plus room and board for apprentice instructors. The next morning I was at Dollar Mountain when the lifts opened. I was wearing my almost-new gabardine ski pants and my brand-new ridgetop skis with bindings I had taken off my old skis. I sported a very nervous smile to camouflage the butterflies in my stomach.

They were all there, the gods of ski instruction that I had read about and watched from afar for so many years: Ski School Director Otto Lang, Assistant Director Johnny Litchfield, and Supervisors Sigi Engl and Sepp Froelich. Emile Allais was there, too. Founder of then very controversial French ski technique, three-time world champion in the 1930s, and a man who could still beat almost anyone in the world on a race course.

I really wanted that job. I wanted to sleep in a warm room for the winter instead of in an uninsulated garage. I wanted to eat three square meals a day for the first time since I'd gotten out of the Navy at the end of World War II. All I had to do was demonstrate my interpretation of how the Sun Valley Ski School taught the various types of Austrian-technique Arlberg turns.

First, there were the very important right turns, and then there were the equally important left turns. I had to demonstrate the snow-plow (now called the wedge or, in kids' classes, "a slice of pizza"), then the stem turn with a lot of weight shift, the stem christie and finally, the turn to end all turns, the parallel christie. I knew that if I got hired I would probably be teaching beginners, so I made sure my snowplow

How I skied in 1948: A combination of California surfer style and imperfectly mastered French technique as taught by World Champion Emile Allais.

was the widest and my weight shift more pronounced than anyone else demonstrating beginning turns.

The ski school tryouts went on for three days. I demonstrated how to climb up, snowplow, walk on the flats, traverse, walk back, do a kick turn to the right and left, make a step turn in one place, carry my skis, put them on, take them off.... I also had to know directions to the men's and ladies' rooms, what the ski school hours were and what was expected of me in the evenings so I could lend atmosphere to the restaurants and bars of Sun Valley. I had to know how to ask for separate checks. Proper procedure. How the system worked.

I tried to ignore the older hot-shot instructors who were snickering at my California surfing style as I demonstrated my turns at the bottom of the Half Dollar chairlift. But by the third and final day, I began to relax a little bit and even hung onto a glimmer of hope that I might be hired. Yes, maybe I could get to sleep in a warm room during the winter for the first time. No more mummy sleeping bags; no more flight boots with squashed mice in them; no more oatmeal and frozen milk breakfasts; no more changing out of my tweed suit and red bow tie in the parking lot in the middle of a blizzard after a date, hanging my suit up in the car and walking back to the trailer in my underwear.

I got the job!

But I was not a model employee. I was an apprentice instructor in an Austrian ski school with a tendency to teach my pupils the French technique when no supervisors were watching. I experimented with building bumps so my pupils would learn fore and aft stability quicker. I sneaked them out on my own time during lunch and taught them to sideslip. I deserved the reputation I was earning of being a renegade.

To my mind, Allais' French technique was a much more fundamental and simpler method of turning skis. Ward Baker and I had been trying to master his technique since reading his book the winter before. First, Emile taught beginners how to sideslip. Next, he taught a lot of upper body rotation. At the midpoint of the rotation you simply contracted your legs. This would release the heels of your skis from the snow so that the rotation of your upper body would be transferred to your skis, and you either turned right or left. Failing any of the above, you simply continued straight on down the hill, accelerating with each passing moment until you somehow creatively bailed out.

One day, in the middle of February, Emile Allais himself took me aside. In his not-very-good English he said, "Otto Lang runs this ski school. He is your boss, and if he tells you to teach kick turns in your long underwear, you do it. He is signing your paycheck. You are very lucky to have a job teaching in the best and largest ski school in America. It is an honor just to be on Otto's staff. Now you go out there and be the best kick turn teacher there ever was. And smile while you are doing it."

I found out later than Emile had his own problems up on Baldy with his advanced students. He was always being assigned rich, but not

"Wherever you go skiing, spare no expense to make your trip as cheap as possible."

very good, women skiers. Most of his English vocabulary he had learned reading the *Saturday Evening Post* during the long boat ride from Santiago, Chile, to San Franciso the previous October. One day, while giving a lady a lesson in powder snow, he was heard screaming at the top of his lungs, "Keep your tits up. Keep your tits up." There wasn't an Austrian instructor in Sun Valley who would correct him.

Still burned in my mind after 45 years is one of the really dumb ideas the ski school clung to. A beginning pupil had to be able to do a good snowplow turn before he or she was allowed to ride a lift. As a result, beginning classes did a lot of climbing. This, of course, made learning a very slow process. It also kept pupils in ski school longer so the ski school made more money. Some pupils who traveled all the way from New York to Sun Valley on the train so they could learn to ski by riding the new-fangled chairlifts were never allowed to ride the lifts the entire week. They spent the whole week climbing up to ski down. They could have done that in Central Park.

One evening I was standing in the Sun Valley Lodge lobby talking to a pupil in my ski school class when I noticed two men who kept staring at me. On my way out they stopped me and introduced themselves.

"Excuse us, but we are from Fox Movietone News. We're in the process of casting two skier/actors for a 10-minute comedy on skis. We think you might fit the role of the pupil in our story. Will you try on this hat and these horn-rimmed glasses?"

"Sure, why not?"

"Where do you work?"

"I'm an instructor."

"Can you look funny while you ski?"

"A lot of people think I always look funny when I ski."

"Can you can get two weeks off from teaching while you ski in our movie?"

"Ask Otto Lang."

They said they would pay me $25 a day and lunch until the picture was finished. I couldn't believe it, but Otto Lang said okay.

Being picked from 32 instructors to star in a ski movie didn't endear me to my colleagues, but it sure sounded good to me. Twenty-five dollars a day was a lot better than the $4 a day I was earning from teaching.

The theatrical short film was shot in black and white on 35-millimeter film, with a camera that must have weighed 60 pounds. Neither the cameraman not the director could ski, so we had to haul everything around on toboggans while they followed on snowshoes.

Even so, I felt like this was a license to steal. Imagine standing around all day in a beautiful place like Sun Valley, making an occasional turn on skis and getting paid to do it!

The 16-volt batteries for the big camera seemed to weigh more than I did. The tripod? Just a little less. And so, day by day and shot by shot we gradually got everything on film the script called for. Jim Patterson played the role of my instructor, and they even paid me to hand-letter SKI INSTRUCTOR on his donated White Stag parka.

But when I found out the cameraman was earning a $100 a day I began to think that this motion-picture business might be a good way to earn a living. The cameraman gave me good advice: "Warren, I've been behind the camera for almost 20 years now. Most people who perform in front of my camera come and go, but I'm still here. If you ever want to go into this movie business, don't be an actor, because everyone wants your job. Very few people want mine." That night I dug out my eight-millimeter Bell and Howell camera with the leather carrying case that I could wear on my belt and kept it with me for the rest of the winter.

To say that we did a lot of exciting things in the movie wouldn't be the truth. Since all of the location moves had to be done on snow-shoes while dragging toboggans with about 300 pounds of stuff, it took forever to get even the simplest shot. From this slow-moving, non-skiing crew I learned how bad it was to miss the powder shot because another skier got there first. I learned that to get that beautiful sunrise between the tree and the clock tower you had to be up before sunrise and ready to shoot.

One of the few scenes that stands out in my mind was one where I had to ski through a split-rail fence. My physics classes in college came in handy for this one. One of Newton's laws states clearly, "Bodies in motion stay in motion; bodies at rest stay at rest unless acted upon by an equal and opposite outside force." That heavy split-rail fence had been at rest in the same spot for about 30 years, and my chest had to set it in motion instantly. At the last minute I suggested that we tape a big piece of wood under my parka and let it hit the fence first, rather than my chest. When I hit that fence at about 20 miles an hour, the big thick piece of wood taped to my chest broke in half at almost the same instant the split-rail fence started moving.

My ribs hurt for a week, but they weren't broken, and I realized that I really enjoyed being an apprentice actor, camera hauler, stuntman and suggester of where to film next. I also enjoyed being paid to do it. My life was taking another small step toward a film career that has so far lasted 55 years.

Laces and Koogi Ties

I f you were lucky when you skied in the 1940s, your soft leather ankle-high ski boots would have had eyes to thread your laces through instead of hooks to wrap them around. Ski-boot laces were made of cotton then, and they would last about 10 days before they began to break on the rough edges of the hooks.

Short of cash and long on ingenuity, I soon got tired of tying knots in my broken 50-cent cotton ski-boot laces every week or so. I figured that if the nylon cord from an Army parachute could keep a soldier from falling to his death, it should certainly be strong enough to keep my ski boots laced up. Parachute cord should also stand up under the rigors of the poorly designed hooks that came on my expensive $17 ski boots.

I got this idea in an Army surplus store in Twin Falls, Idaho. That was when Army surplus stores sold real Army surplus, not the made-in-Taiwan, simulated Army junk you find today. The parachute cord was just lying there in a big barrel, all tangled up like a plate of boiled spaghetti that had turned olive drab with age. It was right between the 20-mm cartridge cases and the cheap wooden replicas of Springfield rifles used for marching practice in boot camp.

You could buy almost anything in that Army surplus store: shovels; hand grenades; 40-mm shells; seven-foot-six-inch ridge-top skis; bamboo ski poles with four-pound baskets; and $3 sleeping bags. Mess kits with three compartments to separate the vegetables, potatoes and Spam were stacked between long underwear and paratrooper boots.

I bought enough olive-drab, nylon parachute cord to cut up into one pair of ski-boot laces for every ski instructor and ski patrolman in Sun Valley, Idaho. However, like the metal ski, the plastic boot and the safety binding that would come along later, my indestructible ski-boot

laces were too radical for any of the old-line Austrian ski instructors in Sun Valley to even think of using, especially because they were olive drab and invented by an American.

I started having nightmares about my $2 investment melting into nothingness with the spring thaw.

On the other hand, I really liked my olive-drab ski-boot laces. They matched my olive-drab, army-surplus ski pants and my olive-drab mittens I had purchased in the same Twin Falls Army surplus store for 50 cents. The mittens had a special place where I could stick out my trigger finger when I was shooting rabbits for dinner.

After the second month of skiing every day and wearing the same pair of olive-drab Army-surplus parachute-cord ski-boot laces, I felt I had done enough testing on my new product—it was time to put it on the market. But first I had to come up with a way to create tips on the ends of my revolutionary laces.

World War II Army surplus parachute cord was made up of woven nylon sheath covering 10 smaller strands of spun nylon. I began experimenting with several methods of sealing the outer sheath and the inner strands. Extensive research and development led me to simply burn the ends with a match. As the end of the nylon cord burned, I would touch it to something while I spun the lace between thumb and forefinger to draw the burning tip away from the object it was stuck to. If I timed it right, the result was a perfectly shaped ski-boot lace tip. If not, I had liquid nylon burning a hole in the table, my pants or the palm of my hand.

Armed with a half-dozen sets of samples of my new time-tested and guaranteed product, I made the rounds of the three ski shops in the Wood River Valley—Pete Lane's, Picard's and Chuck Helm's. In Pete Lane's, after explaining why my hands were covered with Band-Aids, I gave a half-hour sales pitch to Jerry Sidwell, Pete Lane's chief boot salesman. Finally, he said, "I'll try half-a-dozen pair."

I had my first commercial order!

At 20 cents a pair wholesale, and with the cost of materials about two cents a pair, I could see there was good profit in mass producing nylon parachute-cord ski-boot laces. Unfortunately, it turned out to be very hard for Jerry Sidwell to convince his customers to put olive-drab laces in their brand-new $23 genuine imported ski boots. Hunger and necessity being the engine that drives invention, I told Jerry I would see what I could do about manufacturing other colors. It took me a couple of evenings, standing out behind my trailer in the Sun Valley parking lot over my Coleman stove, to boil up a successful batch of Rit Dye, black-nylon, parachute-cord ski-boot laces. I was in the middle of boiling a dozen pairs when I heard a voice behind me say, "What's for dinner?"

How do you explain what looks like a pot of vigorously boiling black spaghetti? Besides, I couldn't tell my ski patrol friend Steve and his girlfriend what I was really doing for fear of industrial espionage. So I put the lid on the pot, turned off the stove and escorted them on a long evening walk.

When I got back, the stuff in the pot had turned to black ice and looked like a biology experiment you might find in the back of your refrigerator. But Pete Lane's liked the new black laces and ordered two-dozen pairs. Over the next two weeks, Pete Lane's sold almost four-dozen pairs of my black laces. Forty-eight pairs times 25 cents equals $12. The total cost of the nylon cord was 76 cents—or an even dollar when I included the cost of the Rit Dye. I had made almost $11 from one store. Fortunately, the ski season was almost over, so I would have all summer to get my new business better organized.

Chuck Helm, who operated the only ski shop in Ketchum, had also sold a couple dozen pairs of my laces, as well as a couple dozen copies of my ski cartoon book. Sitting on the inn front porch one spring afternoon, he asked me if I would paint some of my cartoon characters on the walls of his shop. It was an enjoyable and profitable way to spend each afternoon during the last two weeks that the lifts ran. I really took my time doing these murals, because Chuck was paying me the unheard-of sum of $200 in real cash money. This would give me going-home money and allow me to clean up a few of the debts I had incurred during the winter of skiing. I might even have some money left over that I could use to go surfing when I got back to Los Angeles.

Ward had already left for Manhattan Beach, so I was left to pack up our trailer alone, a time-consuming job for one man. First I had to borrow a shovel to get rid of all the junk that was frozen under the trailer, including a few dozen rabbit carcasses that we had never cooked. Then I had to borrow a pickup truck to take a lot of stuff to the incinerator, knowing I wouldn't be allowed back in California with it. Finally, everything worth keeping was loaded into the car and the trailer, and I made the 900-mile journey to Los Angeles.

That summer of 1948 in Los Angeles I was able to locate some white Navy surplus nylon parachute cord. Taking a real gamble, I bought a $14 roll of it and began coloring experiments in earnest. Between perfecting my new product and spending time with a girlfriend named Lynn who I had met in Sun Valley but who lived in San Francisco, the summer roared by. Lynn made occasional trips to Los Angeles and stayed at her grandmother's place in Pasadena. I soon discovered that the grandmother wanted me to get seriously involved with her granddaughter. We talked a lot about Sun Valley and my dream of building a home there. I had already designed it and run a cost analysis. For my perfect log home, I could spend as much as $800 for the lot and $2,700 for all the materials. Lynn's grandmother offered to loan me $3,500, on one condition—she would hold a mortgage on the house when it was finished.

The check was written and loan papers signed within the week, and I started purchasing plumbing supplies and tools to build the best log house in the Wood River Valley. I even located a shake froe, a rare tool used to split cedar shakes. It was going to be a totally made-by-Warren house.

Two weeks later I had loaded up my plumbing supplies and was heading for Sun Valley with a war veteran friend to help me build my house. As soon as we got to Ketchum in late July, I started looking for a cheap lot. In the process, I met an architect who was just starting to build his own house. Before I knew it, we had struck a deal: I would help him build his house and then he would help me build my house. No cash would change hands. It sounded like a good deal, except that when we had his house about 75 percent finished, he sold it and left town and never did any work on my house.

During September 1948, things really began to cook in the ski-boot lace business. Pete Lane asked me if I could make the laces any other colors besides black and olive drab.

"What color would you like?" I said.

"What colors do you have?" he asked.

"I'll be right back with my color chart."

I jumped on my bicycle and headed for the grocery store in Ketchum. There, way in the back of the store, in between the Brillo pads and the Dye and Shine shoe polish, I found a complete rainbow chart of Rit Dye colors.

I stole the chart!

A couple of hours later I had finished a hand-lettered sign that said, "Miller Boot lace Color Chart." I pasted the Rit Dye color chart under it and rode my bicycle back to Sun Valley and asked Pete Lane what colors he wanted.

"A gross of red and a gross of yellow!"

I had hit the jackpot—an order for 288 pairs of "The Ski-boot laces of the Future." Now I had to burn the ends of each lace one at a time, boil them in Rit Dye over my Coleman stove and then deliver them.

With such a substantial order, it was time for a manpower requirement analysis.

I was dating a lady at the time who was sharing a house with two other girls. The next night we had the first-ever nylon ski-boot lace burning party. I brought along four candles and 400 pairs of laces. We each took 100 pairs and timed how long it took to burn them. When the results were in, I did a quality-control analysis and discovered that if I paid someone two cents a pair to burn the ends, they could easily make as much as a $1.25 an hour. This was when ski patrolmen earned $4 a day.

Dyeing a gross of bootlaces was another matter. Through trial and error, I found out that a gross of boot laces would fit into four one-gallon catsup cans full of water and Rit Dye. I scrounged the cans from the trash bins behind the Challenger Inn and had a friend sterilize them in the dishwashing machine on his night shift. Now I was officially in business.

About this time, I met Flush the Plumber, and he introduced me to

WARRENISM

"I don't want a cheaper lift ticket.
I want an expensive lift ticket that costs less."

someone who would be instrumental in getting my boot lace business going. Flush was installing the rough plumbing for a house down by the Big Wood River. In a nearby hole, digging a septic tank, was Flush's helper, who had just arrived in Sun Valley from the Bavarian Alps.

"Klaus," said Flush to his helper, "climb out of that hole for a minute. I want you to meet that character who lives up in the Sun Valley parking lot. Warren, this is Klaus Obermeyer."

This was the same Klaus Obermeyer who would become one of the most successful ski clothing manufacturers in America.

Flush invited me over to his cabin after work. In his living room, with its rough-wood rafters, I found the boot lace manufacturing facility that I had always envisioned, the perfect place to hang my boot laces to dry after they had been dyed.

Immediately I began negotiating with Mrs. Flush to come up with a price per dozen for dyeing the boot laces. I would furnish the dye and the gallon cans; Mrs. Flush would boil them on her kitchen stove, change the water and add dye for the various colors. She agreed to dye them for two cents a pair. Not counting freight and 25 cents for the Rit Dye for each gross of laces, I stood to make almost 20 cents profit on each pair of my high-tech, high-fashion, color-coordinated, never-wear-out ski-boot laces.

Such a deal!

During this same evening of barbecued venison (poached by Flush the Plumber) and native Idaho potatoes (that Flush had traded for a faucet fix), Klaus showed me what he already had Mrs. Flush manufacturing for him. They looked like the pom-poms high school cheerleaders wore on their saddle shoes. Klaus had several pairs of these pom-poms that he had smuggled into the United States along with his lederhosen when he arrived on the freighter from Germany. He called them Imported Bavarian Koogi Ties. Apparently they were the latest rage in Germany, a substitute for neckties. At least that was his sales pitch, and Klaus had already cornered the market in Ketchum, Idaho. He had sold a dozen of them, in assorted colors, to the Ketchum General Store. The storeowner, who was also the mayor, wore one to a city council meeting as a joke. All of his supporters went right out the next day and bought out the supply.

Mrs. Flush could manufacture a dozen Genuine Imported Bavarian Koogi Ties a day. Fifteen cents worth of yarn and 50 cents for labor went into each Koogi Tie. Klaus sold each one for $3 wholesale. "Tomorrow, the whole world will be wearing my Koogi Ties," Klaus would say.

By now it was early November. The septic tank digging season was about to end, so Klaus and I hatched a plan for a sales trip all over the West. I had promised my parents I would be in Los Angeles for Thanksgiving dinner, so we scheduled the trip around that. We agreed to share gas expenses and sleep in my car to save money. We would call on every ski shop from Salt Lake City to the Pacific Ocean in about 10 days. Our only expenses would be for gas and a few hamburger sandwiches. Klaus could take orders for his Koogi Ties, and I would sell my nylon ski-boot laces.

The frost was everywhere along the Big Wood River, and a dusting of the first snow was on the high peaks as we left Sun Valley late on the 12th of November. I had my Miller Ski Boot lace Color Chart, an order pad and dreams of immediate wealth dancing in my head. Klaus had a dozen different colors of Koogi Ties, a sleeping bag, a pillow, his shaving kit, his skis and boots and a change of underwear.

The very first ski shop we called on, in Boise, Idaho, had been recently opened by a ski racer I had somehow barely beaten in a giant slalom the year before. We had a lot in common and a lot of catching up to do.

"Whatcha been doing since I saw you last?" he asked.

"Did some surfing this spring, moved to Ketchum, rented Austin Lightfoot's garage for $5 a month to store my stuff in. Built a wooden floor over the dirt and spent another $20 for a used oil heater. There's no insulation in it, but just the other night I was able to turn the oil heater up high enough to almost melt all the ice in the pan on top of it. Better 'n living in the parking lot like I have for the last two years, though. What about you?"

"I thought Boise needed a second ski shop, so here I am."

"Klaus, why don't you show him your imports first?"

I knew this guy was a real pigeon when he placed an order for two dozen Genuine Imported Bavarian Koogi Ties. I could see Mrs. Flush getting so busy she would have to subcontract some of the manufacturing to the high school girls down in Hailey.

Now it was my turn. I went through my rehearsed sales pitch with my color chart. Next I showed him my laces from the previous winter with nary a sign of wear with 108 days of skiing. When I finally spread my rainbow of samples on the counter, I knew I had him.

He ordered a gross of them but wanted them in six different colors. Sensing potential inventory control problems, I told him that Pete Lane's of Sun Valley had only ordered red and yellow. So he bought 60 pairs of yellow and took the balance in red.

And so it went. Success at every stop. Spokane, Wenatchee, Seattle.... Everyone we called on ordered at least a gross (144) pairs of my nylon ski-boot laces.

To save time and conserve money, we traveled between cities at night. After sleeping in the car we'd get a shower at the YMCA for a quarter and, all spiffed up, call on the first ski shop that opened in the morning. We developed our list of shops to call on by tearing pages out of the local phone books.

In Seattle we called on all eight ski shops in one day. The biggest shop in Seattle was Osborn and Ulland, where Scott Osborn placed an order for four gross pairs of my laces, one gross each of red, yellow, green and blue, 576 pairs for $144. I could manufacture them for $39.16, leaving me a net profit of $104.84.

Wow, was I excited!

By the fifth day of the trip I had sold 2,500 pairs of my colored nylon laces. I stopped in a restaurant supply house in Seattle and bought two almost-worn-out five-gallon commercial stew pots, finessing the owner out of them for a dollar each because the handles were broken and the bottoms were really bent. I was now fully equipped to manufacture as many ski-boot laces as I could sell, and Mrs. Flush wouldn't have to move the one-gallon tomato catsup cans on and off the stove with one of her husband's pipe wrenches.

Still towing my borrowed luggage trailer, we headed south from Seattle, stopping in Tacoma, Vancouver, Portland and Eugene. We continued to bat 100 percent at every stop.

In downtown Klamath Falls, I sold two-dozen laces to a rod and gun shop owner to use in hunting boots. Klaus unloaded two-dozen Koogi Ties, which he now referred to as German Army Surplus Koogi Ties, on the same gun shop owner, who became the sole Koogi Tie distributor in southern Oregon. He ordered them in colors to match his bowling team's glow-in-the-dark, purple-and-white nylon jackets.

After such a successful day of selling, Klaus bought us dinner in a German restaurant south of town. Wiener schnitzel mit au gratin potatoes, followed by some great Strudel mit schlag. After dinner Klaus and the owner started comparing World War II experiences and wound up trading Koogi Ties for two dinners. Then we headed south to California.

In the San Francisco Bay Area, we placed our products in every ski shop from Marin County to San Jose. A gross of laces here, two gross there. My head was reeling with the mounting success of my revolutionary high-profit deal.

Unfortunately, at this time of my life I knew nothing about volume discounts, C.O.D., credit checks, or 10-percent OEM payments. I had never taken any accounting or business courses in high school or college, focusing instead on astrophysics, calculus, geology, engineering, life drawing and English. I told the shop owners, "I'll ship your laces in a couple of weeks, and you can pay me when you receive them."

"Sure, Warren."

We drove south from the Bay Area, down through the San Joaquin Valley, calling on every ski shop we could find in the local yellow pages. Modesto, Merced, Fresno, Bakersfield and finally Los Angeles. By this time, Klaus and I had figured out that it was safest to sleep in the car in lighted church parking lots. In the mornings we would cruise motel row until we spotted a maid cleaning a unit far from the office. Klaus would put on his thickest Bavarian accent and talk about how he had escaped Hitler's wrath and immigrated to American is search of a dream. "Could my partner and I use the shower in that room you're making up. Here's 50 cents for a couple of towels." If this looked like it was going to fail, Klaus had a great fainting act he could do...German P.O.W., forced to fight on the Russian front, captured at Stalingrad, escaped the Russians...blah blah blah.... Sometimes the maid would feel so sorry for Klaus she'd give him a dollar to help him get started in America.

Klaus and I called on every one of the almost dozen ski outlets in Southern California in only two days, from Tex's in Santa Monica to Forey Neal's Santa Ana Tennis and Golf and east to the Pasadena Ski Shop. I had sold almost 8,000 pairs of my fabulous ski-boot laces, and I was afraid to think how busy Mrs. Flush was going to be, what with manufacturing my laces and Klaus's Koogi Ties. I spent almost $200 for 10 rolls of nylon parachute cord and knew that I should hustle back to Sun Valley as soon a possible.

In Los Angeles, Klaus and I tried to contribute nine poached ducks to the Thanksgiving dinner at my parent's house. Unfortunately, the warm Southern California sun beating down on our car had turned our ducks into smelly roadkill. We settled for turkey dinner and were up early and on our way by 5:30 the next morning.

From San Bernardino to Barstow to Las Vegas, I bought a roll of nickels for the one-armed bandit, played for an hour until I was broke, then feasted at an all-you-can-eat buffet for 95 cents.

We headed north toward Salt Lake City, where Klaus planned to say goodbye. He was going to a brand-new ski resort in the old mining town of Aspen, Colorado. Chicago industrialist Walter Paepke had just built two chairlifts in Aspen, and you could still buy Victorian-style houses for less than $500 each. We didn't have $500 between us, so any real estate deal was out of the question for Klaus. But he was going to get a job as a part-time ski instructor and sell Koogi Ties to both of the ski shops in town and hustle them on the side to his pupils.

After taking even more orders in each of the four ski shops in Salt Lake City, we drove up Little Cottonwood Canyon, where we shoveled out a spot across from the Alta Lodge, backed our car and trailer into it and bedded down for the night. It snowed non-stop for the next two days while we skied together in the deep powder and slept in the back of my Ford in the snow bank. The third morning we got up and started digging the car and trailer out of what had become a very large snow bank. By noon we started driving down to Salt Lake City. There I said goodbye to Klaus at the bus depot, left him standing there clutching his small bag of worldly possessions, including his sleeping bag, skis and his sample line of Genuine Imported Bavarian Koogi Ties.

Alone now, I started driving north to Sun Valley, anxious to get my ski-boot lace factory set up.

I had sold almost 8,000 pairs of laces at a profit of 19 cents a pair. Wow! That house I wanted to build next spring was getting closer to reality. I had spent a lot of Lynn's grandmother's money to cover start-up costs for my new business, and she was starting to ask me about making payments, because six months had gone by and I had not as yet started my house. My brain was spinning with cost analyses, production capabilities, time and motion studies, and shipping logistics and methodology. Labor supply and management philosophy were finally in place, so I could complete the bottom-line performance analysis.

Before leaving on the trip with Klaus, I had moved most of my worldly possessions into Lightfoot's garage with its new wooden floor and oil heater. Unfortunately, the garage wasn't insulated, so the temperature inside was usually colder than the temperature outside, unless you were within a foot of my almost new oil heater. I thought I could improve the situation by nailing the canvas tarpaulin I had brought from Southern California to the rafters, thus creating an insulated ceiling. I was wrong, but the tarpaulin, a much-splattered painter's drop cloth, at least lent an air of abstract art deco to my new Idaho digs.

"Let's see: I'll put my bed over there, the Coleman stove over there, and I'll build my painting easel against the east wall. That will give me enough room to paint signs when I'm not working on my ski-boot lace business or out painting murals on injured skiers' casts..."

Of course, I went skiing whenever possible. Then, as now, my priorities were based on the snow conditions of the day. I knew everything would eventually get done.

Unexpectedly, I tried out for and got a job as an instructor with the Sun Valley Ski School. Thirty dollars a week, a meal ticket, a ski lift ticket and a lower bunk in a chalet. I had already gotten my new Northland skis in exchange for painting a couple of signs for Pete Lane's shop. The repair and rental shop was in the basement of the Challenger Inn, where no one could ever find it. So I painted some of my cartoons, along with a lot of directions, on two pieces of four-by-eight plywood and put them over the steps leading down to the repair shop. Of course I painted my colored nylon ski-boot laces on all of the skiers in my cartoons.

Christmas was coming soon, and I had to get my ski-boot lace orders manufactured and shipped out, finish a half-dozen different sign painting commitments I had and keep the oil heater turned way up in my garage apartment. Many nights it was way below zero when I was painting signs in my combination art studio, ski-boot lace manufacturing plant and warehouse. It was so cold some nights that I would turn my two-burner Coleman stove way up and put it on the floor under the drawing table so I could keep my body working. Once, to meet a deadline, I tried painting a sign in the lobby of our instructors' chalet. No dice. Two instructors didn't like the smell of turpentine mixed with the wine they were drinking.

A typical laid-back day in my life as a ski instructor went like this. Up by 6:30, a quick breakfast, and then I would coordinate boot lace orders with Mrs. Flush. How many had she dyed for me the night before? When could I pick them up so I could package and ship them? Then I would go to the employee cafeteria and line up two or three people on my employee roster for the next nightly ski-boot lace tip burning party. (I had to stay ahead of Mrs. Flush.) For the burning parties, I had to make sure I had enough candles, but not enough wine.

I made the mistake early on in my career of supplying all the wine the tip burners wanted to drink. Between inhaling nylon smoke and ingesting the cheapest wine the State Liquor Store sold in gallon bottles, everyone at the party would be an automatic no-show the next morning. It took about 10 burning parties to find a staff of reliable tip burners who wouldn't get drunk. I also had to think about ordering more rolls of white nylon parachute cord far enough in advance, so it could be shipped up from Los Angeles on the train. It was a two-night, three-day trip on the Union Pacific via Salt Lake City and on to Green River, Wyoming, where it would be transferred to a westbound freight train and travel to Shoshone, Idaho. There it was transferred again on the daily train to Ketchum.

The ski-boot lace orders kept pouring in.

After all the phone calls, interviews and scanning the morning mail, I would get into my ski school uniform and hurry over to the ski school meeting place, where I would be assigned my class of never-having-skied-before pupils. The teaching hours were from 10 to 12 and from two to four.

I quickly learned that beginning skiers were very easy to talk into private lessons at $4 an hour. I did this because I was given 25 percent of any private lesson money or $1 for each hour I taught. If I had a private lesson to give, I would do that from 12:15 to 1:15, then grab a hamburger to eat on the bus, so I could get to the Post Office and pick up new ski-boot lace orders. Then I'd hurry back to the ski school meeting place to teach from two to four. Between four and dinnertime, I would stop by the hospital and check out the new broken legs and maybe paint a cartoon or two on a fresh cast. If I were lucky, I'd have a date with one of my pupils and take her to the Challenger Inn for dinner. If we got along well and she was very understanding, a second date was sometimes a possibility. At that point I would invite her to my deep-freeze garage apartment where she could sit shivering in her fur coat while I painted yet another sign. Or maybe we'd stop by the Flush Family Lace Factory to see if they were meeting my production schedule. I was a very busy ski instructor.

It seemed as if almost everyone who went into a ski shop would walk out with a pair of my laces. I had sold them to almost 75 different outlets around the country. Today a product like that would be called a fashion trend. I have no idea how many laces I sold that winter, but Pete Lane's alone was selling almost 200 pairs a week. Thirty percent of the skiers in Sun Valley were replacing their cotton laces with my guaranteed-for-a-year, color-of-your-choice nylon laces.

Mrs. Flush was working my five-gallon nylon-lace-dyeing pots to the limit, and we were somehow making all of our shipping deadlines and filling our orders and reorders. By then Mr. and Mrs. Flush had taken on the day shift of ski-boot lace-end burning to keep up with the demand of phone-in orders. Together the husband and wife team was making as much as $24 a day.

I didn't know it at the time, but the business was falling apart in the record-keeping department. The closest bank to deposit all my money was 12 miles away in Hailey, and I didn't have time to drive down there and make deposits. I didn't know that I could have banked by mail. I was so dumb about money I thought you had to deposit your money in person. So I put the money in the mail and sent it to my mother in Los Angeles so she could bank it for me in person. In the spring my records indicated that I had sent $5,600 in checks and money orders to her. I'd spent all the cash I'd received.

When I returned to Los Angeles after the snow melted and the lifts closed in the spring, I stopped by my parents' house to find out which bank my money was in so I could buy the rest of my house-building materials.

"Gee, son, I don't know where you got your figures, but I've only gotten less than $900 from you all winter."

I had no money-order receipts, no profit-and-loss statements, no accounts receivables ledger, and no shipping records. What I had was the memory of my mother spending time in the county jail for forgery when I was 10 years old.

I'd been had by my own mom.

It looked like my house-building project would have to be put on hold for a while longer.

Squaw Valley, 1950:
A Season of Firsts

In the spring of 1949, there was talk among the ski instructors at Sun Valley that a new ski resort was going to be built in California. It would have a revolutionary chairlift that could carry two people at a time sitting side by side; it would be the third chairlift in California (the other two were at Sugar Bowl and Mt. Waterman).

None of us could imagine how two people on seven-foot, six-inch skis could load onto a chairlift at the same time. But then, none of us could see how Howard Head's revolutionary metal skis could ever replace handmade hickory skis, either.

So much for our foresight.

Emile Allais was teaching at Sun Valley at the time and had been asked to be the director of the Squaw Valley Ski School. As an instructor of beginners in the Sun Valley Ski School, I was big believer in Emile's revolutionary French technique. It had to be good, I figured, because he had used it to become three-time world champion. I decided to apply for a job at Squaw Valley.

That summer I worked in a factory in Los Angeles testing air mattresses. Just about the same time I got fired for falling asleep on the job once too often, Emile answered my application: "Be at Squaw Valley, California, one week before Thanksgiving, and you will be paid $125 a month and room and board."

I was there on time.

The story of Squaw Valley began before World War II when Wayne Poulsen and Marti Arroge purchased all of the land in the valley. After the war, they sold Alex Cushing 25 acres (at a very low price), with the proviso that he build a chairlift to get the resort started. That

Squaw Valley's revolutionary double chairlift had so much room it could occasionally double as a triple.

chairlift, Number One, went up to the base of the headwall and stopped there. Cushing also built two ropetows just east of the lodge, one for experts, of which there were very few, and one for beginners, of which there were even fewer.

On the long slow ride up the chairlift, there were two unloading ramps, one near Tower 10, the other near Tower 20. The ramps were designed for about 25 or 30 feet of snow. At the beginning of the season, when there was little snow, skiing down those steep ramps on wooden skis with dull edges and no release bindings was a hair-raising experience. I think that's how extreme skiing got started.

When I arrived just before Thanksgiving with my brand-new 16-mm movie camera, I was very enthusiastic about Squaw Valley. Wayne Poulsen was selling lots ranging in price from $800 to $1,100, the more expensive ones with a view of both the valley and Squaw Peak. He had very few buyers, however, because none of us had any money.

The lodge (since burned down) slept about 20 or so people in rooms that could only be reached by a wide set of stairs right up out of the dining room. The employee housing occupied a semi-circle of buildings to the north. We called it the barracks, because the buildings had come from a Naval training center near Reno. Men slept in one building and women in another.

Most of the time.

There was nowhere for us to go when we weren't working, so between Thanksgiving and Christmas, Jack Simpson and I built a bar and lounge under the lodge front porch. We assumed we would be paid at least 50 cents an hour for our work, but when it was done we got nothing beyond our salary. Management's attitude was, "Ski school instructors only have to work four hours a day teaching, while the rest of the employees work eight, so why should you get paid extra?"

Our ski school had four instructors: Dodie Post, Charlie Cole, Alfred Hauser and myself. On a good day, we would each have one pupil.

Prior to opening day, Thanksgiving 1949, there was only about 18 inches of snow as far down the mountain as Tower 20, with dirt and rocks below that. However, enough snow had blown into one of the bowls to ski on, so that's where Emile trained us.

At the snow line there was a small muddy lake east of Tower 20. With enough speed it was easy to coast across its frozen surface and then climb back through the rocks to Tower 20 and get on the lift. Thus was pond skimming invented.

Late one afternoon, just before the lift closed (and it would close whether you were riding on it or not), I was coasting across the lake when I broke through the ice. Fortunately, the water was only knee deep, but I quickly discovered that it was very difficult to untie my long thongs under two feet of muddy water, get my boots out of my skis, reach down and retrieve the skis from that freezing cold water, then thrash and crash the rest of the way to shore through ice that was too thin to support me. The 15-minute ride down on the lift was freezing cold, but listening to Emile laugh at my stupidity made it seem a lot longer.

Dinners for the staff consisted mostly of macaroni casserole and, for dessert, carbonated Jell-O. That's right: Carbonated Jell-O. Alex Cushing had brought his butler out from Boston, who ended up as the cook in the lodge when he wasn't butlering. Money was short, so he carbonated the Jell-O to make it go farther. That's how ski-resort food got its start.

Squaw Valley's double chairlift was state of the art at that time, but there was no one on staff with state-of-the-art experience to operate it. Avalanche control was non-existent. After one five-day storm, five feet of snow stacked up on the valley floor. When the lift operators tried to start the lift, the cable ground to a halt. No amount of coaxing could get it moving.

Climbing the liftline later that day, we discovered that Tower 22 had been bent over by a big avalanche, and the cable was caught under the sheaves. Emile, Stan Tomlinson, Arnie Madsen and I talked it over and decided that we would try to unbolt the tower from the ground so it might tip over—and then the lift could run again.

When there was only one bolt left holding the whole mess together, I stupidly volunteered to knock the final bolt out of place. I tapped the bolt and jumped back. Nothing happened. I tapped it again and jumped back. Still nothing. After about 38 taps and jumps, the bolt fell out and the tower just lay there, hanging over the cable in dynamic suspension.

We then tied a long rope to the bottom of the tower, got it swinging back and forth, wider and wider until it fell off the cable. Then the cable, with all the chairs, flew up into the air until it was about 100 feet above the ground. That created a wave in the cable that shot down the hill, around the bullwheel and back up the other side.

We skied down the hill and told them to start up the broken lift. They did, and it ran as advertised. Tower 22 never was replaced, which was the start of creative lift repair.

There was a lot of room on the double chair, so when an old girlfriend of mine from Sun Valley showed up for some lessons with her girlfriend, the three of us rode up together, perhaps creating the triple chairlift.

During lunch hour one day, the kerosene stove in the ropetow shack got too hot and burnt the shack to the ground. The lower sheaves of the expert ropetow also burnt, and for a few days that ropetow just lay in the snow. By the time someone got around to fixing it, four feet of new snow had covered it up.

To make money to buy film for my brand-new 16-mm movie camera, I took black-and-white still photos of people sitting on the porch during lunch hour. At night I would go down to a darkroom at Deer Park, process and print the pictures and then try and sell them for a dollar the next day. If the woman in the picture was not the guest's wife, I sold the negative for five dollars, inventing, in my own way, the fine art of ski resort guest extortion.

Snow grooming had not yet been invented. Some of the moguls lasted all winter, because they just kept getting bigger and bigger.

Sometime during the middle of January, after a quiet dinner at the only restaurant open in Tahoe City, a group of us went over to the Tahoe Tavern to talk to some of the guests. (They happened to be the only guests at the Tavern at the time.) These particular guests were trying to promote ski trains from San Francisco to Truckee, with a transfer to a spur line that ran from Truckee to Tahoe City, where you could stay at the luxurious Tahoe Tavern.

The scheme was never realized. Now the railroad track is no more. Neither are longthongs and leather ski boots. But there is one thing that never changes at Squaw Valley: The feeling of making turns with good friends in new powder snow, when the sun is out, and the sky is so blue you can see almost all the way around the world.

FIFTY YEARS WITH
SKIS AND CAMERA

The Education
of a Filmmaker

I n 1935, at the age of 11, I realized the rich financial rewards offered by the "film" business when I discovered several 400-foot rolls of highly flammable 35-mm film in the deep dark recesses of my grandfather's basement. The film was at the bottom of a nail barrel, right next to the wine my grandfather was fermenting in a big earthen crock. Grandpa occasionally sipped a bit of the grape, and my Christian Scientist grandmother always pretended not to know.

In the near darkness of the basement, I secretly, and I thought very skillfully, cut and rolled short pieces of the nitrate film into tight, one-inch diameter rolls. A one-inch diameter roll of 35-mm nitrate film, if tightly wound and then lit with a match, will burn very slowly and generate enough foul smelling smoke to completely empty a school room. For only five cents, my friends and classmates could purchase one roll of my flammable film wrapped in plain white paper, secured with a band from a chewing gum wrapper. Each roll of film had a hand lettered label that said, "STINK BOMB."

It was my first entrepreneurial adventure.

It was also my first travel adventure. I got to travel to the superintendent's office in the back of a police car.

With the profits from this venture, I purchased my first camera for 35 cents, a genuine "Univex Camera with sports viewfinder." Each roll of black-and-white film that I purchased and exposed, including developing and printing, cost 10 cents, which is what I earned in a day working in the neighborhood grocery store.

About six months later, with eight or 10 rolls of picture taking experience under my belt, I shot two rolls of film on a backpacking trip with my Boy Scout troop. At my next Boy Scout meeting, my patrol leader

wanted copies of all of the pictures I had taken of him. He wanted to prove to his parents that he really had gone backpacking with our Scout Troop and hadn't hitchhiked to Newport Beach for a weekend party.

I charged him an extra 20 cents for his copies. Now I had enough money to buy and process my next two rolls of film. Without realizing it, I was learning how to build a business with plowed-back earnings instead of borrowed capital.

At age 12, I took on a Saturday Evening Post magazine route, earning 15 cents a week. Then, in junior high, I started delivering the *Hollywood Citizen News* six days a week and earning a $1.50 a week. Not counting the time it took to commute by bicycle to my paper route, I was now earning 15 cents an hour. This was during the Depression, when most adult wages were 10 cents an hour—if you could find a job.

All during high school (1939-1942) war raged in Europe; just before I graduated, the Japanese attacked Pearl Harbor. I was barely 17 years old. Somehow I enrolled at the University of Southern California and stayed for the next year and a half. Tuition was $5 per unit, plus books and lunch. To pay those bills, I polished floors in the library, starting at four in the morning and finishing in time to get to my eight o'clock classes. I had another job working in the student union serving lunch. Both these jobs paid 25 cents an hour, and at the Student Union I also got free lunch.

Skip ahead to 1946. I had just been discharged from the U.S. Navy and was walking down Market Street in San Francisco, when I was attracted by a motion picture camera in a store window. Within half an hour, I had endorsed my $100 mustering-out check to purchase my first movie camera, an 8-mm Bell and Howell with a single lens. There was even a guaranteed exposure guide on the side that made taking movies virtually foolproof. Along with the camera came a genuine leather case, so I could carry it on my belt. The store owner even threw in a free roll of black-and-white film.

With the additional money I had saved up while in the Navy, I bought a homemade four-foot-wide, eight-foot-long trailer with a kitchen in the back and a bedroom that could sleep two people. I would live in this trailer with my surfing buddy Ward Baker, and together we would travel and ski almost every day all winter. We camped out and lived free in the parking lots of the West's finest resorts and skied more days than most people get to ski in a lifetime.

Returning to Los Angeles, we had 22 rolls of eight-millimeter movies of our season-long ski trip, including cameo shots of celebrities like Gary Cooper, Groucho Marx, Darryl Zanuck, John Wayne, Claudette Colbert and Ernest Hemingway. It wasn't long before I was entertaining our Southern California surfing friends with those movies.

While I was showing our ski films to my surfboard riding friends, I started taking surfing movies at Malibu and San Onofre. My plan was to show those films in Sun Valley when Ward and I returned the following winter.

Soon total strangers began to invite me to dinner.

"Oh, and by the way," they'd say, "will you bring your projector, your screen and your ski movies with you?"

About the tenth time I showed our ski movies in exchange for a macaroni and cheese dinner, I began to realize that I was covering up some of my bad photography with remarks that people laughed at. That was the birth of my "mean spirited humor." Destiny and a dash of entrepreneurship, mixed with unpleasant memories of my poverty-stricken childhood, were already shaping the future direction of my life.

I was already 23 years old.

Then came my first promotional coup. During our first winter in Sun Valley, a writer/photographer had taken some photos and written a story about us living in the Sun Valley parking lot and subsisting on frozen jack rabbits. The story had appeared in a national magazine. Armed with that magazine article, I visited several Southern California trailer manufacturing companies and used a very simple sales pitch: "Here's what Ward and I did last winter, and here is some of the publicity we got. We're going to travel and ski again all next winter, and we're going to enter a lot of ski races. We can get this same kind of publicity for *your trailer company*. How would you like to have it featured in a national magazine parked in Sun Valley, or Yosemite or maybe in front of the Hotel Jerome in that brand new ski resort called Aspen?"

At the fifth trailer company I visited, I ran into an old friend that I had surfed with for years.

"Hey, why not?" he said. "You can use one of our new models. Just return the trailer to us in the spring."

It pays to have friends at the top. Actually, my friend was assistant inventory control manager, and he got fired when his boss found out he had loaned us the trailer for the winter, but by that time we were already living in it in Idaho.

1961-62

SCHEDULE OF SHOWS

OCTOBER
16—Salt Lake, Utah (East Hi)
18—Stamford, Conn. (Civic Aud.)
20—Colorado Springs, Colo. (Perkins Hall)
21, 22—Denver, Colo. (Phipps Aud.)
23—Salt Lake City, Utah (East Hi)
25—Reno, Nevada (State Bldg.)
26—Danville, Calif. (Walnut Creek Country Club)
28—Bend, Oregon (Hi School Aud.)
29—Eugene, Oregon (Roosevelt Jr. Hi)
30—Corvallis, Oregon (Hi School Aud.)

NOVEMBER
1—Spokane, Wash. (Civic Aud.)
3—Yakima, Wash. (Yakima Hi Aud.)
4—Wenatchee, Wash. (Wenatchee J. C. Aud.)
5—Bellingham, Wash. (Bellingham Hi Aud.)
7, 8—Vancouver, B. C. (Pendar Aud.)
9, 10, 11—Seattle, Wash. (Eagles Aud.)
12—Portland, Oregon (Benson Tech Hi Aud.)
14—San Francisco, Calif. (Morris Aud.)
15, 16, 17, 18—Los Angeles, Cal. (Wilshire Ebell Theatre)
19—San Diego, Calif. (San Diego Hi Aud.)
23—Ogden, Utah—(Ogden Hi Aud.)
25—Syracuse, N. Y. (Civic Aud.)
26—Rochester, N. Y. (German Club Aud.)
27—Garden City, N. Y. (Garden City Hi Aud.)
28—Detroit, Mich. (Detroit Inst. of Arts)
29—Troy, N. Y. (Civic Aud.)
30—Worcester, Mass. (Mechanics Hall)

DECEMBER
1—Pittsfield, Mass.—(Berkshire Museum)
2—Hanover, N. H. (Dartmouth)
3—St. Paul, Minn. (Civic Aud.)
5—Fitchberg, Mass.—(Fitchberg Hi Aud.)
6—Hartford, Conn. (Bushnell Memorial)
7—Cambridge, Mass. (Cambridge & Latin Hi)
8—Lynn, Mass. (Civic Aud.)
9—New London, N. H. (Hi School Aud.)
11—Philadelphia, Pa. (Town Hall)
12—Duluth, Minn. (Washington Jr. Hi Aud.)
13—Wausau, Wis. (Hi School Aud.)
14—Traverse City, Mich. (Hi School Aud.)
15—Lake Forest, Ill. (Lake Forest Hi Aud.)
17—Idaho Falls, Idaho (Civic Aud.)

DECEMBER—(Continued)
18—Fresno, Calif. (Junior College Aud.)
26—Yosemite, Calif. (Village Pavillion)
29, 30—Sun Valley, Idaho (Opera House)

JANUARY
3—Boise, Idaho (Hi School Aud.)
5—Truckee, Calif. (Hi School Aud.)
7—Marysville, Calif. (Marysville Hi Aud.)
8—Palo Alto, Calif. (Belmont Theatre)
9—Carmel, Calif. (Grammar School Aud.)
10—Bakersfield, Calif. (Hi School Aud.)
11—San Gabriel, Calif. (Mission Playhouse)
14—Santa Ana, Calif. (Santa Ana Hi Aud.)
15—Long Beach, Calif. (Lakewood Country Club)
16—Redondo, Beach, Calif. (Redondo Hi Aud.)
17—Dallas, Texas (Civic Aud.)
19—Ligonier, Pa. (Ligonier Hi Aud.)
21—Milwaukee, Wis. (Shorewood Aud.)
22—Chicago, Ill. (Lane Tech Hi Aud.)
23—Buffalo, N. Y. (Kleinhans Music Hall)
24—Grosse Point, Mich. (Detroit Country Club)
26—Cadillac, Mich. (Cadillac Armory)
27—Boyne City, Mich. (Boyne Falls Theatre)
29—North Adams, Mass. (Drury Theatre)
30—Melrose, Mass. (Melrose Hi Aud.)
31—Quincy, Mass. (Quincy Hi Aud.)

FEBRUARY
2—Lake Placid, N. Y. (Lake Placid Club)
5, 6—Montreal, Canada (West Hi Aud.)
8—Portland, Maine (Portland Hi Aud.)
12—Boston, Mass. (N. E. Univ. Aud.)
13—Boston, Mass. (Harvard Club)
14—Ann Arbor, Mich. (Hi School Aud.)
15—Boulder, Colo. (Macky Aud.)
16—Aspen, Colo. (Wheeler Opera House)
18—Stanford, Calif. (Stanford Univ.)
19—Ontario, Calif. (Chaffey Hi Aud.)
20—Whittier, Calif. (Whittier Hi Aud.)

MARCH
6—St. Anton, Austria
7—Zurs, Austria
9, 10—Davos, Switzerland
12—Courchevel, France

How to Become an Overnight Success

T here were good days and there were bad days, but for four decades I traveled more than 100,000 miles a year with two cans of film under my arm, a tape recorder and a suitcase full of dirty laundry. I did as many as 106 live narrations each fall and winter, in as many as 106 different cities. Along the way I slept in as many as 212 different hotels and motels during one year.

For those four decades, the routine was pretty much the same.

I would get a wake-up call at about 5:30 a.m. in the motel I was staying in, grab a taxi to the airport, or walk to the bus depot, or drive my car to the next town for the next show. Sometimes the trip between the shows would be an hour or two, sometimes clear across America, from Los Angeles to Boston on the midnight plane. But it would almost always be seven shows in seven cities in seven days from the middle of October until just before Christmas, then all through January and the first two weeks of February. Then I'd start traveling to film the next year's movie.

I always tried to arrive at the theatre at least an hour and a half before show time to make sure that the promoter had the right projector, screen and sound system. More often than not, one or more of those three components would either be broken or missing. So in addition to my own tape deck and film, I always carried tools and spare parts. That way I could usually jury-rig my way out of any problem.

The first thing I would do when I arrived was renew my acquaintance with the janitor or the stage manager. Next I would haul out some rickety old table that I had hidden backstage the year before, set up my tape recorder and check sound levels. The next stop would be the projection booth high above the balcony—if they had one. Then I

WARRENISM

"Be kind to your kids, because someday they will choose which run to make you ski down."

would clean the gate on the projector, which in many cases had not been cleaned since the year before—when I had done it myself.

The audiences were different every night, both in attitude and attendance. Such as one night in Pennsylvania at a suburban high school auditorium.

I knew I was in trouble when the promoter invited me to have dinner with him at 7 before an 8 show. I knew I was in really serious trouble when I arrived at the school and found the auditorium dark. At 7:15, the janitor finally showed up to let me in. Still, I wasn't too worried because I had a guarantee of $175 for the evening, $25 more than my usual fee in 1955. It was a real scramble to get all the equipment ready for the 8 showing, but by 7:45, when the promoter showed up with what was left of his six-pack, I had everything set up. He quickly sold eight tickets for a $1.50 each to the eight people who had been waiting in line.

That was it! Eight people to fill up a 1,300-seat auditorium. I wandered out into the parking lot to see if we should hold up the show for late arrivals. There were none.

I was chatting with the policeman out front who had been hired to handle the crowd, when an elderly lady strolled out of the darkness with her dog. She was the geometry teacher at the school and lived nearby. She had seen the lights and wandered over to find out what was going on. I invited her and her dog and the policeman to see the show.

Inside, I wandered around the auditorium introducing myself to the eight people who had paid to see my latest ski film starring Stein Eriksen, Christian Pravda, Dick Buek and eight-year-old Jimmie Heuga. I invited them to come sit down front, then climbed up on the stage and talked to the 1,290 empty seats and the 10 full ones (not including the geometry teacher's dog). I told a few stories about the film and then asked the janitor to turn out the lights and the 13-year-old projectionist to turn on the projector.

When the house lights went off, the projection room electricity went off. So during the next few minutes of total darkness I chatted with the 10 people in the audience—11 if you count the promoter who was popping the cap on the last remaining bottle in his six-pack. I thought about the advice I had been given in 1950, the year I showed my first ski film. That time there were 37 people in the Sun Valley Opera House, a theatre that seats 300. The old-time vaudeville performer who was running the theatre gave me a bit of advice that would see me through a lot of the ups and downs of show business. I still think about that 50 years later.

1) Always entertain the people who showed up and feel sorry for the people who didn't.

2) You will work all your life to be a success overnight.

3) Never stop working.

The Way it Was

I t's November 5, 1999. Fifty years of traveling the world with my skis and camera have gone by faster than the speed of a downhill racer.

In 1946, when I started making my first 8-mm ski movie in Alta, Utah, there were only 15 chairlifts in North America. Oregon, Washington, New Hampshire and Canada had one each, California and Colorado had two each, Utah had three and Idaho had five. The then high-speed chairlifts at Sun Valley, Idaho, could only haul 436 people per hour. Today a state-of-the-art six-passenger chairlift in Washington can haul 2,600 people per hour.

There have been a lot of changes in the sport of skiing since 1946. The one I miss the most is that until about 1970, I could go to almost any ski resort in the world and find plenty of powder snow for the skiers in my movies. Since then ski equipment, ski technique and high-capacity ski lifts have changed the sport so that you have to be in the liftline by seven in the morning if you want to ski untracked powder snow.

I lament the decline of available powder, because it has always been the best part of my time spent in the mountains. It has also been what my movie audiences enjoyed the most. However, I am happy that so many more people can enjoy what I have enjoyed since I first went skiing in 1937.

The first time we filmed powder-snow skiing in a helicopter with Mike Wiegele in Blue River, B.C., in 1969, Mike didn't even have two-way radios, because he didn't have any employees. He had rented a small three-place Bell helicopter, and that entire winter he only had 13 people show up to ski with him. Today thousands of people fly in from all over the world to enjoy untracked powder snow skiing. A lot of the reason for that increase is the change in snowriding equipment.

In Alaska, you can go night sking all day long.

In the spring of 1949, I was teaching at Sun Valley, Idaho, when I first met Howard Head with his aluminum skis. He showed up with a dozen pairs of the shiny new metal skis, and only one or two instructors would even try them. Most of us had the attitude that "if God had wanted skis made of aluminum, He would have made aluminum trees."

Howard Head was willing to try anything to make the sport easier, because he was such a lousy athlete. As most everyone did in those days, Howard had a hard time turning seven-foot-six-inch hickory skis. Within a week of his arrival in Sun Valley, all two dozen pairs of his supposedly revolutionary skis had broken or fallen apart. Four or five years later, he had those problems worked out, and his skis revolutionized the sport of skiing. Turning a pair of Howard's metal skis was a lot easier than turning a pair of traditional wooden skis, and, like Henry Ford's cars from the previous generation, you could buy them in any color you wanted as long as it was black. But you had to have a good job to be able to afford Howard's skis—they cost $85 a pair. In 1953, you could still buy almost any other make of wooden skis in the world for under $30.

In the early 1950s, our soft leather ski boots were locked down to your skis so tightly that in the event of a bad fall there was a good chance your body would revolve but your foot wouldn't. This phenomenon ruined more than one ski vacation. Some of the best ideas in safety bindings, or release bindings, as they're called today, were hatched by skiers lying in hospital beds with broken legs.

In early December 1956, I was invited to ski and film at Wilmot, Wisconsin, on a hill that was less than 200 feet high. At the time there wasn't a single snowflake east of the Rocky Mountains, and yet right in the middle of hundreds of acres of green pastureland, alongside the Wilmot ski lift, was a patch of white stuff that looked just like snow.

Walt Stopa, the owner of Wilmot, had jury-rigged some galvanized iron pipe with a lot of fittings so he could blast water under high pressure against other pieces of pipe, creating tiny water droplets. A rented air compressor shot high-pressure air into the water droplets that then flew out into the freezing air, which froze before they hit the ground. It was the first time I had seen artificial snow (later called man made snow). Walt Stopa didn't invent snowmaking, but that day in 1956 was my first experience skiing it and filming it.

Today, permanent snow guns are installed alongside ski trails, and as soon as the temperature is low enough, a computer automatically turns on all the pumps, the water, the air compressors—and sometimes very good quality snow starts covering the ski runs.

A month after I filmed at Wilmot, I was in Aspen, Colorado, filming Herbert Jochum. He was cruising along in about 14 inches of delightful powder snow that had fallen on top of huge moguls. As we got halfway down the mountain we heard the sound of a tractor. An employee of the Aspen Skiing Corporation was "grooming" the moguls with wooden two-by-fours bolted to the treads of a small Oliver tractor. Both Herbert and I got very upset. We felt the tractor operator was ruining the mountain. Today, every major resort has at least a dozen snow-grooming machines that work all night every night.

Nineteen forty-nine was the start of dramatic changes in the ski industry when the third chairlift in California was built at Squaw Valley. I taught skiing there that first winter when they operated their one chairlift and two ropetows. That third chairlift in California was the start of an exciting new trend in skiing, because it carried two skiers in each chair instead of one.

During the last 50 years a lot has also changed about travel to ski resorts. My first trip from Los Angeles to Aspen was in 1953 in my panel delivery truck. The roads were narrow, two-lane and ice-covered. Snow tires had yet to be invented, so the 1,200-mile trip took almost 35 hours.

When I finally arrived in Aspen, I got to stay in the Hotel Jerome for free because I was making my third feature-length ski film and had agreed to include the Aspen Winterskol parade. The parade consisted of the ski school instructors marching with their skis over their shoulders followed by the ski patrol hauling a toboggan with wagon wheels on it and three pickup trucks decorated with signs. Leading the parade was a flatbed truck with the king and queen of Winterskol sitting on five bales of hay. The snow was great that day, so very few people watched the parade.

Flying to ski resorts in the 1950s was difficult because most of the airline employees had never seen a pair of skis. Often I had to tie my skis to the legs of the three back seats in the DC-3. That airplane wasn't pressurized, so they couldn't fly over the highest mountains in Colorado. Instead they would detour north over Wyoming and then south to Denver. The parking lot back then at Stapleton Field in Denver was in a muddy field across from the main terminal.

The long drive to Aspen from Denver always seemed to include being stuck behind three or four 18-wheelers traveling at five or six miles an hour over Loveland Pass in a blizzard, then a slip and a slide (this was before snow tires) down to Dillon (before the dam and the lake) and then a long climb up over Vail Pass behind more slow-moving trucks. There were only a few farmhouses where Vail now stands. Recently, one of the original lots in Vail with a 35-year-old house on it sold for $9 million. The new owner tore the house down to build something bigger.

After 50 years of filming skiing and 61 years of making turns in snow, people are still asking me when I'm going to get tired of skiing.

I was asked that same question when I flew to Anchorage, Alaska, in a Constellation in the late 1950s. The morning after I showed my ski film at Anchorage High School, a bunch of us got into someone's pickup and drove out to Turnagin Inlet on a dirt road. Everyone was talking about what a great place Alyeska would be for a ski resort. We parked the car alongside a trapper's cabin, climbed to the top and started filming. The magnificent backdrop of the tide rushing into the inlet is a sight you have to see, especially since they now have a lot of lifts and Alyeska is one of the few places in the world where you can go night skiing all day long.

For me that desire to make more turns on snow never goes away. It's still an adrenaline rush, especially when I'm going snowriding where I've never gone before.

Skid Chains

Long before the invention of mini-vans, SUVs, air bags, ABS brakes and radial snow tires with studs, someone invented that archaic piece of unmanageable hardware called the tire chain or, as its sometimes called, the skid chain. A good pair of chains used to cost about $10, and if you skied in the Sierra or Cascades, they were indispensable. Even today if you drive up from near sea level to go skiing in California, Oregon or Washington, you pass through climatic zones where the rain turns to slush and then to snow. When the storm is severe, the Highway Patrol posts a guard and won't let you drive on up to the ski resort without putting on your chains. Long ago I learned to obey the Highway Patrol in this matter, sometimes putting on chains even before it was required. Here's how my diligence was rewarded on one occasion.

Some years ago I was trying to sell a short film to my friend Dick Kohnstamm at Oregon's Timberline Lodge. I flew to Portland from Los Angeles, arriving about midnight, just in time to get the last available rental car, and then started up toward Mt. Hood. At about the 3,200-foot elevation, freezing rain convinced me to stop. I spent the night in the Notel Motel in the small town of Rhododendron, where the sign out front said, "Morally clean, luggage required."

The next morning, six inches of new snow covered my rental car. Rather than wallow in the mud at the chain-control station up the road, I decided to put the chains on right there in the motel parking lot. No big deal. I laid the chains out on the ground behind the rear wheels and backed the car over them, just as I had done hundreds of times before. Then I wrestled the chains up over the tops of the tires, hooked everything up, and was ready to go.

The rest of the drive to Timberline Lodge was without incident. The parking lot, however, had two-and-a-half feet of new, wet snow. Typical Northwest powder. But with my skid chains on tight, I had no problems. It was even fun making first tracks in the parking lot. But when I came to a stop I found it was impossible to open the car door— the snow was that deep.

Because this was a sales trip, I was wearing a sport coat, slacks, necktie and loafers and carrying my briefcase. Unable to open the car door, I climbed out through the window and immediately sank up to my knees in new wet snow. After loafer-packing the snow around the door, I managed to get it open. Then I grabbed my briefcase, rolled up the window, and wallowed toward the lodge.

Discussions about the film took a couple of hours, followed by a two-hour lunch. I said goodbye to Dick and headed for the parking lot. Now I could barely see my rental car. It looked like it had snowed another six inches. Ten minutes later, having scraped the windshield as best I could and acquired two solidly frozen feet, I was ready to charge out of the parking lot. With those top-of-the-line skid chains, I figured I had all the traction I needed. But the car wasn't ready to leave. Nothing I could do would make the car move. I rolled down the window and discovered that the front wheels were spinning.

That's when I realized this was a front-wheel-drive rental car, and I had put the skid chains on the back wheels!

I sat there for a few minutes with the engine running and the heater on high while I tried to figure out how to get my chains moved to the front wheels without help. Through the fiercely blowing snow I spotted a pickup truck with its engine running. I got out and staggered a couple of hundred yards through three feet of snow. I could see the driver of the pickup was a typical mountain person. He had a broom sticking up in the back of his truck. A shotgun and a trout rod nestled in a rack in the back window. A black labrador was sitting in the passenger seat wearing a red bandana, and the driver had a long, full beard. He was eating a sandwich and reading a local tree-hugger environmental magazine.

I knocked on his window. He rolled it down about three-quarters of an inch and said, "I been watchin' ya. See you're stuck."

"I sure am. Will you help me get unstuck?"

"Where ya from, fella?"

"California."

"Thought so." Then he quickly rolled up his window.

I hollered above the howling wind, "Would 20 bucks get you to help me get my car unstuck?"

I waited for what seemed like three hours until he slowly rolled his window down again.

"Tell you what, mister. For two 20-dollar bills, I'll hitch a rope to your car and drag you out to the plowed road. But only if you promise me one thing."

"What's that?"

"When you head down that highway, make sure you go back to California and never come back. Up here, we is skiers!"

Dinner with the Governor

I t was 1963, the second ski season for l'Oeuf, the gondola in Chamonix at La Flégère. Each gondola car was painted a different primary color and, from a distance, they looked like Easter eggs gliding up and down the mountain in the spring sunshine. I had named them "The Dangling Easter Eggs" in my 1962 film. The lift went up the sunny side of the valley, to one of the best views of one of the most spectacular mountains anywhere in the world, the massive tumbling icefalls of the north face of 15,000-foot Mt. Blanc.

I had extensively filmed "The Eggs" the winter before and had shown the film in theaters all over America. I had now returned to rendezvous and ski with my new friend, the president of the resort. We met at Le Chapeau restaurant for the standard two-and-a-half-hour French lunch. Pommes frites, steak, salad—and introductions all around the table.

"Warren, I'd like you to meet the Governor."

"Hello, Governor," I replied.

Lots of people are called governor. No big deal. He was tall, dark-haired, handsome and had a very beautiful wife. Unfortunately, neither could speak English, and my French language skills consisted of being able to order an omelet. I would find out, after a very long lunch and half a dozen runs in great corn snow, that they were also excellent skiers.

It was late spring and, because of its southern exposure, the lower section of La Flégère was without snow. So I rode down in the gondola with the Governor, his wife and the president of the resort. As we neared the bottom, the president said, "The Governor would like you to come to dinner at his home while you are here in Chamonix."

"Sure, why not," I replied.

WARREN MILLER 02

"How about Wednesday night?"

Three days later, after a long day of filming, I took a shower, slathered my face and the top of my head with sunburn grease to ease the pain, and started the long, winding drive down to Annecy.

Two hours later, in a pouring rainstorm, I arrived on the outskirts of Annecy. There, I located a petrol station that was still open and, with the Governor's address clutched in my hand, I used my expert sign language to converse. Ten minutes of arm waving later, I was given directions with what appeared to be a certain amount of reverence.

Soon, in my dim headlights through the slanting rain loomed a big iron gate, probably 40 feet wide and 10 feet high. To its right was a sentry box that resembled a phone booth with a peaked roof and no windows. Standing out of the rain was a soldier wearing a gold-buttoned

WARRENISM

"Ski weird when you're young so when you get old people won't think you're crazy."

coat with epaulettes. He was holding a heavy rifle with a fixed bayonet. Professionals were guarding this guys house!

I knew I was in trouble because I was driving a Volkswagen with German plates, and I couldn't speak but a few words of junior-high French. "S'il vous plait? Le mansion Monsieur Governor?"

"Oui."

"Monsieur Miller. Le Guest."

" Oui. Oui!"

Marching stiffly to the far side of the gate, he leaned into it, and it swung slowly open. I was now staring down 600 feet of gravel driveway, flanked on either side by immaculately trimmed shrubbery and trees. The house in the distance resembled a 47-room luxury hotel I once stayed at in Zermatt.

As I coasted my rent-a-wreck to a stop behind a long line of limousines, I knew I was in real trouble. It was dawning on me that this guy really was the Governor, and I might be under-dressed.

Let's see: I'm wearing a red-and-yellow ski parka over a brown-and-beige tweed suit, a red bow tie with white polka dots and a nylon wash-and-wear shirt that is sort of pressed. I guess I shouldn't have worn my après-ski boots. The sheepskin lining is going to get awfully sweaty in there at dinner.

I knocked on the massive wrought-iron-and-cut-glass front door. When it swung open, it revealed a highly polished marble-floored foyer with a pair of gently curving stairs that were 12-feet wide going up each side of the foyer. The butler, clad in tails and white gloves, was visibly shaken by my appearance. He started talking rapidly in very hushed tones of what sounded like Norwegian with a French accent. He proba-

Fingerprints on the Tram

The other night I was on my hand and knees on the living room floor putting my electric train together (a wonderful replica of a European train my wife gave me a couple of years ago). Once I had it put together and running around, under and through the various pieces of furniture and the Christmas tree, I sat back and started thinking of some of the train stations I had been in in Europe. Brig, St. Anton, Zermatt, Kufstein, Kitzbühel and Mittendorf, to mention a few. Nowhere else in the world has the machinery to transport people in general and skiers in particular been elevated to such a sophisticated level as it has in Europe.

Probably the world's most sophisticated ski lift is the Aiguille du Midi tram in Chamonix, France, which opened in 1955. Early one morning, many years ago, I stood there waiting for it to start up. Loaded down with a rucksack full of film, cameras, lenses, tools to repair broken things in the rucksack, batteries, electrical cables and a peanut butter sandwich or two, I was excited—and so were the four skiers I would be filming, who waited there with me.

An overweight ticket taker, clad in an ancient, faded and very dirty parka appeared. "Bonjour," he said, inhaling deeply on a foul-smelling cigarette of Egyptian tobacco.

Our tickets punched, we noisily climbed the two flights of stairs in our ski boots to the waiting cable car and stood in the corner that would provide the best view. After a few minutes of pushing, nine more people than the car was designed to hold crammed into its beat-up interior, and the door slid shut. It felt like there were 10,000 people in a car designed for 60, most of them with foul-smelling Egyptian cigarettes dangling from their lips. The windows of plexi-glass had been scratched opaque by the thousands of skis that had been leaned against them during the many years of the tram's trips up and down the mountain.

The ride up that first section of the tram was a somewhat normal cable-car ride. Unfortunately, at the end of the ride it was first-in-and-last-out. When we finally got out and climbed two more flights of stairs and squeezed into the next cable car, my rucksack and tripod were resting uncomfortably against the knees of a garlic dealer from Milan. The combination of garlic in his clothes and another of those Egyptian cigarettes at close proximity was almost more than I could handle.

But when the second tram began to move silently upward, we entered another world. The impossibly jagged Aiguille du Midi loomed almost vertically above us as we glided silently through the sky almost 2,000 feet above the rocks, the cable supported only by top and bottom towers. In the distance, Mt. Blanc rose to more than 15,000 feet, its flanks buried by glaciers, some of them more than 500 feet deep. A plume of blowing snow stretched off to the northeast from the summit in a thin line against the dark-blue morning sky. Inside the battered tram, everyone now spoke in whispers as if in church.

Actually, we were whispering because we were afraid the cables holding us up wouldn't last another trip. In the corner, a gray-haired woman, unperturbed, rode skyward to work. All day she would serve wonderful food at 13,000 feet in the mountaintop restaurant, and at the end of the day she would ride down again. For her it was all in a day's work.

I glanced down and noticed a hole where the floor of the car had been worn thin by the thousands of ski and climbing boots tramping in and out during the many years the lift had been operating. Seeing that hole, the four famous skiers with me lost some of their bravado.

The tram began slowing for its arrival at the top terminal, its motion guided by some unseen hand in the bowels of the engine room. Stopping gently, it quickly emptied. The other people groped their way

through a long dark tunnel hollowed out of the solid needle of granite. I stayed behind to watch the battered red tram, its roof covered with grease and dirt, once again drop like an elevator toward the lower terminal. It occurred to me that the view as the car dropped might make a spectacular shot for one of my movies. I could open the hatch in the roof and hold the camera outside to get the shot. Someday, I thought, I'll do that.

I groped my way through the long tunnel, across the bridge and out the other side of the granite needle. An eight-mile-long glacier curved away to the left below us and disappeared into a fog bank. A rope barrier stretched across the top of the three flights of stairs that led down to the glacier. A sign said, "Ferme!" There would be no skiing today.

It looked like I was going to get those shots riding down in the tram sooner than I expected.

Five cups of tea, two croissants and a lot of marmalade later, the five of us were standing in an empty tram car with the roof hatch open. I would have my chance to run my camera and create that feeling of falling through space. One of my four skiers spoke French, and a chair mysteriously appeared for me to stand on. Now I could get my head and shoulders above the roof.

"Are you ready?" someone asked.

"Yes."

Suddenly three sets of hands grabbed my legs, hoisted me up onto the greasy roof, the hatch slammed shut and the tram began to drop. I grabbed hold of anything I could find to hang onto. Riding down on that greasy roof, 2,000 feet above the rocks and ice, I felt like I was hanging onto the wing of an airplane coming in for a crash landing. But I got the shot.

Twenty years later, a friend of mine came back from Chamonix and said, "Warren, your fingerprints are still on the roof of that tram. But they told me to tell you they finally put a new floor in the cabin."

Cathedral of the Gods

The sky above the village was slowly changing from black to gray to the pale blue of dawn. In the street below my apartment, the apprentice baker peddled by on his bicycle, dwarfed by his huge wicker basket full of delicious-smelling rolls for the hotel down the street. I had already been up for half an hour packing all my camera gear in a rucksack.

At 7 a.m. I arrived at the helicopter pad with our guide, our three skiers from Idaho and my cameraman. As I climbed in and buckled up, the anticipation in the air was so thick you could cut it with a knife.

The pilot, who only spoke French, started throwing switches and doing things that caused the turbine engine to scream its high-pitched whine. The pilot did whatever he was supposed to do with the controls, the tail lifted up, and we began to move forward and claw our way upward in the cold, thin high-mountain air.

Because I was paying for everyone's ride, I got to sit in the front seat to the left of the pilot and keep my movie camera running during most of the flight. In the back seat sat our Zermatt guide, Ricky Andermatten, my other cameraman, Don Brolin, and skiers Bob Hamilton, Pat Bowman and Jon Reveal.

As the magic machine climbed torward Theodel Pass that led from Zermatt to Italy, the sun was already etching beautiful, angular shadows across the untracked snow and the glacial ice fields that in places are more than 500 feet deep. To our right, the Matterhorn assumed its rightful role as the alter in this vast Cathedral of the Gods.

Barely 15 minutes after we left the village, we landed gently in deep powder snow on the northeast shoulder of Monte Rosa. What had taken us 15 minutes in the helicopter would have taken 24 hours if we

had climbed it on our skis.

During the next six hours, under the direction of Don Brolin and myself, Bob, Pat and Jon leaped over crevasses, rapelled down ice blocks and carved endless turns in untracked powder snow.

Our guide, Ricky, kept us alive with his knowledge of where the ice bridges and crevasses would be, where we could ski and where we would die.

Gradually, Don and I began to get the sequence "in the can." We would film the three skiers making a dozen or so turns and then ask them to stop. Don and I would then put our gear back in our rucksacks and ski down to somewhere below them, stop and set up our cameras for another angle while they would wait for us to compose the shot. Then, following Ricky's expert advice, I would tell them where to turn and where not to turn.

At about 2 or 3 p.m., Ricky said, "I have a great surprise for you guys. "Follow me, but be sure to stay in my tracks."

He then skied on down below us for three turns and disappeared down a slope that led right into a crevasse, hollering "Follow me!" John, Pat, Bob, Don and I slowly and timidly followed him. I have always been suspicious of surprises on high mountain glaciers, especially when people disappear into a crevasse! So I took longer than usual to put my camera away, and then I slowly sideslipped down to join them.

At the bottom of the powder snow slope that led down into the crevasse, everyone was standing in silent awe. Except for me: I was scared to death! As my eyes slowly got accustomed to the darkness, I became even more frightened. We were standing inside the beginning of a half-mile-long, 40-meter-wide, 20-meter-high tunnel of ice. At the far end, the sun was sending brillant slivers of fractured rainbows in every direction. Beside us, a 10-meter-wide, one-meter-deep river of pale grey-green, almost white icy water, rushed noisily by.

Overhead, the massive ice blocks of the glacier were leaning together, forming a true Cathedral of the Gods. The slanting ice walls were 40 or 50 feet high and had been undercut along their base by the swiftly flowing river.

Ricky was the only one who didn't appear to be scared when he said, "We can ski along this ice ledge by the river. It's only about a meter wide, so be careful. Be sure not to slip and fall into the river. If you do, you'll get sucked under the ice and drown before I can rescue you."

This seemed like an appropriate time to ask Ricky what I thought was a very logical question: "What makes you think this ice won't cave in on us while we're down here?"

He had a logical answer: "Warren, what makes you think it will?" Ricky had probably been down here before, he knew what he was doing, and he wasn't going to risk his life just to show off for us.

As I inched slowly along on the black ice ledge, I was spellbound by the hanging icicles, the dripping water, the pale grey-green water rushing by and the many different colors of the ice. I was really scared by the occasional rumble and thunderous explosions coming from the movement of some other block of ice somewhere else in the vast glacier. The noise of its movement was amplified and transmitted all the way to where I cowered.

About half a mile later we emerged into the brillant light at the end of this unbelievable Cathedral of the Gods—more beautiful and, for me, more religious than any of the cathedrals I have visited in a lifetime of world travel.

When we finally began sidestepping to get up into the brilliant sunshine and powder snow on top of the glacier, it was a lot later than I thought. We had spent over an hour traversing only a half mile under ice that was at least 400-500 feet thick. Now we would have to hurry so we could catch the last gondola before it left to take us down to the village at six o'clock. Led by Ricky, we took off in a long, high-speed traverse for the last mile or two.

Ahead of us and slightly off to the right, the Matterhorn showed us yet another of its many moods in the late afternoon sun. To the left of this incredible mountain was the Theodel Pass that leads to Italy, and a little further to the left was Monte Rosa. I could still see our tracks etched by the late afternoon sun, tracks that we had filmed eight hours and five or six miles earlier.

Ricky, Jon, Pat and Bob had very quickly skied away from Don and me. We were laden down with our rucksacks full of about 50 pounds of cameras and tripods. I also had an extra 20 birthdays to carry

"I'd give up skiing if I didn't have so many sweaters."

around, which always adds a certain amount of weight to a day's work on the glacier. I was lurching along, last in the wet tracks of slushy snow, when a flash of light caught my eye way off in the distance near the top of Theodel Pass.

I stopped and was barely able to make out two tiny dots carving figure eights in the late afternoon corn snow. They were headed for one of the mountain huts to spend the night.

It was a beautiful sight. So I took off my rucksack, unhitched my tripod, set it up, got out my camera, mounted it on the quick-release, hooked up the battery belt, spun the prism so I could see through the viewfinder, focused the lens and then zoomed it to the maximum focal length telephoto available, 285 millimeters.

What I saw through the lens was truly unbelievable: The tracks they were leaving in the backlit corn snow were almost black.

As I was reaching for the on switch on my camera, a thought occurred to me: "I've been recording scenes like this since 1949, so I could share them with millions of people. Why not save this one just for me?"

So I didn't turn on my camera. I just watched these two skiers make 109 turns while my own party of skiers traversed on ahead to the gondola. If I missed the last gondola, so be it.

No one will ever see that beautiful scene. Nor will anyone ever see any pictures of the interior of my own private Cathedral of the Gods.

I never did turn my camera on, but those two images are forever etched in my mind.

The Killy Caper, Part 1

In August 1968, after six months of negotiations and pre-production planning, I found myself standing barefoot in my jockey shorts in waist-deep freezing-cold water. We were at a mountain lake at the base of Mt. Ruapehu, on the North Island of New Zealand. I was the only one in the film crew dumb enough to wade out and help guide in a small amphibious plane that was delivering French ski champions Jean-Claude Killy and Leo Lacroix to our production crew for the first month of a six-month ski odyssey.

Our original production plans had been to film in Portillo, Chile. Lack of snow made us switch at the last minute to Mt. Ruapehu, where I had never directed a film before.

And I have never directed one since.

The weather in New Zealand was as bad as our accommodations were good. We could sit in the hotel lobby eating lobster paté, fresh trout or peanut butter and strawberry jam finger sandwiches while sipping tea and looking out under the rain clouds to see the sun shining four or five miles away. My cameraman, Don Brolin, and my son, Scott, together with a crew of 12 other people, sat around day after day watching it rain. We moped around like the professionals we were, while the first episode of our TV show was going way over budget with each passing hour.

Meanwhile, only 10 miles away, standing in the bright winter sunshine, the smoking volcano, Narahoe, beckoned to us, "come on over here and ski and film."

We talked a lot about trying to film skiers skiing its steep windblown ridges. That would mean hiking seven miles to the base of the mountain and hauling 100 pounds of camera gear every mile of the way,

just to get to the snow line. Once there, we would have to climb for every single shot of every single ski turn.

At about 3:30 p.m. on the afternoon of the 13th consecutive rainy day, while sipping a pot of tea and having one more fresh lobster paté sandwich in the hotel, Narahoe erupted with a spectacular cloud of smoke and steam, blowing rocks and ashes downwind as far as 12 miles. Fortunately for us, the prevailing wind was away from the hotel. The hot ashes and rocks, however, left an ugly black slash down the eastern slope that now stood out in sharp contrast to the white snow.

Every afternoon for the next three days, Narahoe violently erupted between 3:30 and 4:00, as though triggered by some accurate geological time clock. By now, we were getting desperate for footage of Jean-Claude and Leo doing anything that had to do with skiing.

I began to think, "Why not try to hire a helicopter that could fly us over to the summit of the volcano early in the morning? We could ski and film until about 3:15. The helicopter could then pick us up somewhere on the windward side of the mountain and fly us home so we could escape before the scheduled daily volcanic eruption."

We hired a helicopter, and the next morning Don Brolin and I lifted off at 7:30 with the pilot, who was wearing a tweed sport coat over a white linen shirt with a button-down collar and a tartan-plaid wool necktie, heavy woolen pants and brown and white saddle shoes. No leather gloves, silk scarf or crash helmet for him; this guy was so confident of his own ability that he was dressed as though he were going downtown to a Saturday night dance. He had made no emergency plans whatsoever. This gave us all an immense amount of confidence in his ability.

Dumb!

Ten minutes later, he dropped Don and me off on the rim of the smoking volcano and quickly lifted off to bring Jean-Claude and Leo up to us on his next trip.

It was truly awesome to stand on the lip of an active volcano and look down into the smoking and steaming crater, to stand there on the ash-covered ice and snow and see pieces of the earth moving around down there. We were almost overpowered by the stench of sulfur dioxide and wondered if it would blow up before we finished filming at 3:30, or even while we still stood there.

We planned to film on the windward side of the volcano. That way, if it did blow up while we were up there, the rocks and ashes would blow down the other side of the mountain instead of falling down on top of us.

I felt perfectly safe. Sort of.

We spent all day filming Jean-Claude and Leo skiing very aggressively against a background of the smoking crater. At about 2:30, the ground began to shake every few minutes with increasingly sharper and more violent earthquakes.

Don and I talked it over. Relying on my one semester of Geology 1-A in college, I made the decision to stay.

"I think it'll be an hour before it kicks off its daily explosion."

When we landed on the volcano's rim this one last time, the incredible roar blasting out of the crater had increased to such a volume that it was impossible for anyone to hear my directions when I was shouting a foot away from their ear.

We couldn't even hear the helicopter we were climbing out of.

I had to use sign language.

WARRENISM

"If you don't do it this year,
you'll be one year older when you do."

We all knew that this would be our last filming and skiing decent of Narahoe, so Killy and LaCroix really did a number on the available terrain.

For years I have said, "Skiing is like dancing with the mountain."

That day we were all skiing and dancing with death.

During our third camera setup, Don and I looked at each other and then took our cameras off the tripods because the ground was now shaking so much we couldn't get a steady shot. For the last few shots of Killy and Lacroix, we had to hand-hold our cameras. As they carved turns, they were framed against the growing cloud of steam, sulphur dioxide gas, ashes and the occasional rocks that were starting to be blasted skyward.

We only needed one last shot of the helicopter landing and picking up Leo and Jean-Claude to complete the sequence. I was shocked, though, as I watched it come in for a landing down below us, and disappear into a dense fog bank. It disappeared at least three miles away from where we were supposed to be picked up, way out on the flat. By this time my French had improved to where it was only 98 percent sign language; Jean-Claude and Leo's English was about the same. But we all understood the sign language of survival. The two of them didn't even slow down after the last shot; they raced right on by us and disappeared into the dense fog, headed for the now distant sound of the helicopter.

Don and I quickly threw our cameras into our rucksacks, tucked our tripods under our arms and followed their ski tracks down to where the brush and trees began to stick up out of the snow. Somehow, Jean-Claude had found a path through the underbrush to where the helicopter was waiting. By the time we got there, he and Leo were already strapped in and the pilot motioned to us that he would be back to pick us up in a few minutes.

Let's see, that would mean he would be back at about 3:45, or 15 minutes beyond the volcano's normal explosion time. I sure hoped the wind would keep blowing from the northwest so that we wouldn't get buried under its daily shower of rocks and ash. In the thick fog I didn't know how the pilot, who was still wearing his tweed jacket and dancing shoes, was going to be able to find us.

He showed up as he said he would, and on time, too. We quickly lashed our skis onto the landing gear, put our tripods and rucksacks full of camera gear on the floor of the small, three-passenger Bell helicopter, while he adjusted the controls and lifted off. At about 200 feet above the ground, we broke out of the fog and could see the hotel sitting off in the distance, still under a rain cloud. Off to our left, Narahoe's volume of smoke had increased dramatically while we had been nervously waiting in the fog for the chopper's return. The pilot gave us the thumbs up and, just at the same moment, the biggest eruption we had seen in a week blew out of the crater where we had been standing and filming less than 25 minutes earlier.

When the "Jean-Claude Killy Skis New Zealand" episode of our new TV series was edited and presented to the networks for approval, their Ethics and Practices Committee made us change it all around. They claimed that no one would believe the sequence, because no one would be dumb enough to ski down the side of an active volcano.

We were that dumb, and we have the film to prove it.

The Killy Caper, Part 2

fter the 1968 Winter Olympics in Grenoble, France, my film company won the rights to produce a TV series featuring triple gold medalist Jean-Claude Killy. The detailed itinerary called for us to visit a different country or ski resort every week for 13 weeks. So much for well-laid plans.

Our first stop was Mt. Ruapehu on the North Island of New Zealand, where we sat in the rain for three weeks as I contemplated how much money I was losing. We finally got enough film in the can by skiing on a nearby active volcano that was blowing up every afternoon between 3:30 and 4:30. Then we chartered a DC-3 for a bumpy ride to the South Island to film the 12-mile run down the Tasman Glacier on 12,349-foot Mt. Cook, New Zealand's highest peak. The DC-3 landed on a field that was no more than a flat strip of grass.

An hour later, as we drove toward the Mt. Cook Hotel, the scenery was shrouded in low-hanging clouds. When you can see the Southern Alps, they are a rugged range of snow- and glacier-covered mountains larger than the Swiss, Austrian, Italian and French Alps combined. The wind and rain beat incessantly against the underpowered and overloaded van as we slowly gained altitude. Ten minutes later, wet sticky snow forced the ancient windshield wipers to grind to a halt.

The New Zealand weather, never predictable, again refused to cooperate with our tight production schedule. With 17 people in our crew, the Killy TV series was already way over budget because of the North Island debacle. For five days we waited out the rain and sleet at the Mt. Cook Hotel, where we had to wear coats and ties to lunch and dinner. After dinner on the fifth night, I took a long dejected walk,

thinking about how much money I was losing per hour. It had been 18 years since I borrowed $100 each from four friends to start my film business. Now I was completely dependent on my client to take care of the weather contingencies, and I was scared.

It was then that the weather finally began to clear. By the time I returned to the hotel, the Southern Cross was shining brightly in the middle of a spectacular canopy of stars. I started to get excited. Maybe tomorrow would be the day.

I had hired a small three-seat Bell Helicopter that was piloted by a bounty hunter named Mel Cain. The first time we met, he flew his helicopter right through the open doors of an airplane hangar where we were cleaning our camera gear. At the time, an out-of-control deer population in New Zealand was devouring all the natural grasses, which in turn created serious erosion. Government officials were offering a bounty of $3 a tail, and Mel had bagged 900 in the last month alone. I knew that the Tasman Glacier was out of bounds for helicopter landings, but Mel assured us that he had permission to land anywhere he wanted in Mt. Cook National Park.

Because the Bell only carried two passengers at a time, I flew up early the next morning with Killy. My other cameraman, Don Brolin, came up on the second flight with Leo Lacroix, Killy's teammate on the French National Team and a champion skier in his own right. Sometimes Mel let us out on slopes that were so steep he had to anchor the landing gear in snow while the helicopter was still hovering. We would then climb out on the skid in our ski boots, inch our way along it and attempt to gently step off into the hip deep powder snow. Then we would ski the length of the glacier in a foot or two of untracked powder, past 100-foot-deep crevasses and 70-foot-high cobalt blue ice blocks that looked as though they could tumble over at any time.

We lost all track of time while setting up and completing each shot of the two best skiers in the world. Collectively, the four of us had more adrenaline pumping that day than most people generate in a lifetime. It seemed as if only an hour had passed when the light began to fade into evening. There wasn't a cloud in the sky, yet it was suddenly getting dark. The sun had gone down, the day was over and we couldn't get any more powder shots.

It was then that Mel spoke up. "It's already too late to fly you out in pairs. It'll be pitch black by the time I can get back up here, and I won't be able to find the other two."

WARRENISM

"A fool and his money are invited places."

His solution to the problem seemed simple at first. "Two of you can ride inside the helicopter and the other two can ride on the outside, tied to the landing gear." This meant flying a three-seater with five people, plus four pairs of skis and more than 100 pounds of camera equipment. That's a heavy load for taking off from the side of a mountain at 10,000 feet.

Mel suggested flipping a coin to determine who got to ride inside and who had to ride outside, but I reminded the group that I owned the film company. "The three of you can flip to see who rides on the outside."

Don "won" and prepared to hop inside while Killy and Lacroix bravely faced their fate. We tied two pairs of skis with the bindings down on each of the landing skids to create two platforms. We then tied Killy and Lacroix on these platforms like a couple of dead deer.

Now it was up to Mel to somehow get the overweight Bell off the ground. He revved the engine until the tachometer screamed against the red line. The machine struggled and shook until it finally got a few feet off the snow, where it hovered for a moment before slamming back down with a thud.

It was getting darker by the minute as Mel fine-tuned the controls and gave the engine a slightly different mixture of fuel and air. This time, the helicopter rose four feet in the air, hovered for a few seconds and came down gently.

After five or six of these four-foot-high flights, I noticed that Mel was leapfrogging his way slightly downhill and to his left. He was moving 15 or 20 feet with each jump.

"Why are you heading this way?" I shouted.

"There's a cliff over there, and I'm trying to time my short flights so when we get there we can fall off and hopefully get airspeed," Mel hollered back. "Once we do that, we'll have enough forward speed so I can get us back to the hotel."

I didn't like the word "hopefully."

But Mel timed it exactly right. We fell off the cliff and gained airspeed, with our cargo (the world's two greatest skiers) lashed to the skids like dead deer. We made it safely back to the hotel, where we landed in total darkness. That night at dinner, dressed in our coats and ties, Killy called it the way it really was. "A mountain is like a beautiful woman. You can go to her as often as you want, but she will only give you what she wants.

"Today, she gave us our lives."

Hot Dog Roast

Years ago, in Vancouver, British Columbia, a young man approached me after my show and said he wanted to star in my next ski movie and be famous for the rest of his life. I gave him the stock response I'd used on so many other ski-movie wanna-be's: "What can you do that's different from turning your skis left and right or just going straight and leaping off a cliff?"

He caught me by surprise when he said, "A friend and I have bought a $10 Army surplus asbestos fireproof suit. It even includes a complete asbestos facemask and helmet. Here's our plan: I'll wear the suit, my partner will pour gasoline all over me, then he'll light me on fire, and I'll ski down the hill in flames and jump off a big cliff."

That sounded like a pretty good idea to me, so I said, "You do that, and I'll make sure I have a camera crew there to make you world famous."

Exactly 61 days later the drama unfolded on an overcast day at Squaw Valley, California, under the watchful eye of the local ski patrol. My ace cameraman, Don Brolin, had hired eight or 10 extra people to help him with fire extinguishers, first aid supplies and to run additional cameras. Don wisely figured that if the young men had bought the fireproof suit for only $10, it probably had seen better days and might have a leak here or there.

Our soon-to-be-famous hot dog skier had selected just the right rock to jump off and had laboriously hauled 15 gallons of gasoline up to where he would start skiing down in flames. By his calculations, it would take five gallons of gasoline per attempt. He decided that the suit could probably last for three flaming trips.

The day before the jump, he and his assistant had practiced the

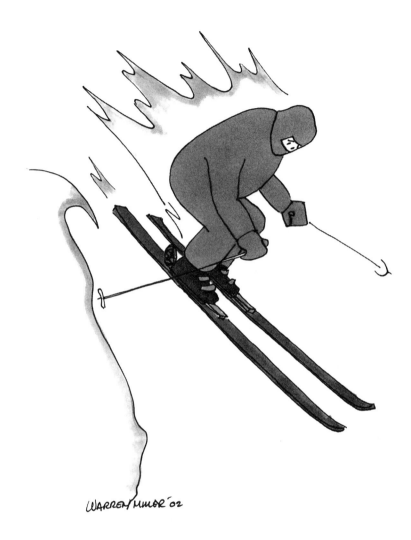

countdown by dousing the suit with water a dozen or more times. Unfortunately, the suit built up so much ice in the cold mountain air that it was hard for him to bend it as he crouched to spring off the takeoff.

The day finally came.

"Cameramen ready?"

"Yes."

"Fire extinguishers ready?"

"Yes."

WARRENISM

"There is never a wrong time to make a right turn, and there is never a right time to make a wrong turn."

"Asbestos Man, are you ready?"

A mumble emerged from inside the suit, then a wave and a thumbs up. The gasoline started flowing over his helmet, down over his shoulders and back, his chest, and then a little extra shot of gasoline on his skis.

"Get ready for ignition."

"WHOOOOOSH!"

An explosion roared across Squaw Valley, and everyone instantly had second thoughts about the wisdom of this hot dog roasting. But with three cameras rolling and flames leaping six or eight feet high, he shoved off. Before he had skied 15 feet, the viewing port of his fireproof helmet fogged up, so he couldn't see the takeoff. He jumped anyway, because he had to get down the hill to where the men with the fire extinguishers were waiting. The world's first barbecued hot dogger flew about 100 feet and crashed in flames. As the flames were dying, our crew of minimum-wage firemen spewed fire-retardant over the suit, and Asbestos Man emerged unscathed.

Over lunch everybody worked to solve the fogging problem. In the end they rigged up a breathing tube that went under the hot dogger's armpit. That way he'd be breathing toasty-warm but smelly armpit air instead of cold mountain air, and the faceplate wouldn't fog up.

Or so they hoped.

After lunch he suited up again. His assistant suggested more gasoline. While more gasoline was hauled to the top of the in-run by three off-duty bartenders, the cameramen practiced their pans so they wouldn't miss, and the firemen took practice squirts of fire-retardant foam.

Everything was ready.

"Pour gasoline!"

"Now the second can!"

"Roll cameras!"

"Ignition!"

"WHOOOOOOOOOSH!"

This time the flames were so high he looked like an airplane going down in flames. Looking through a clear faceplate and breathing warm armpit air, he flew 100 feet through the air—and still crashed in flames. The five firemen converged on him spraying foam while he slid another 100 feet and finally rolled to a stop.

His first question after he took off his still-smoking helmet: "Will I be world-famous?"

"Sure," said cameraman, Don Brolin, "but in that full suit no one will recognize you."

My Father Hates You

I was standing on a catwalk one day when someone skied to a stop alongside me and said, "You're Warren Miller, aren't you?"

"Yes."

"I just had to tell you that my father hates you."

This seemed to be a different way to start a conversation with a stranger.

"Why?"

"Let me ride up on the lift with you, and I'll tell you the whole story."

This guy had all the right moves, the right equipment, the right amount of duct tape on his faded gloves, and the elbows of his parka were a little worn. I could tell right away he was between 25 and 35 years old, because he had the signature mustache of that age group that's looking for identity and isn't sure how to get it.

On the lift he told me his story.

"When I was a little kid, my dad used to take me to watch you make your personal appearances with your ski films in the Ford Auditorium in Detroit. You always showed up with a new film the night before Thanksgiving, and the first two or three times I went, I'd sit in my dad's lap and scream and shout like everyone else did. I didn't know why I screamed, but it seemed the thing to do.

"I remember when you showed Vail on the screen the first year it was open and you said, 'Get out here and discover it before everyone else does.' My dad made Christmas reservations for us the next morning.

"My two brothers, my mom and I complained all 1,200 miles from Detroit to Colorado, but dad drove nonstop in our station wagon. We had to stay clear down in Glenwood Springs and drive back and forth every day to ski, because there was only one hotel in

Vail, and it was sold out. Dad didn't tell us this until we drove right by Vail that first night.

"But when my dad skied down the catwalks from Mid Vail with me between his legs, I became completely hooked on skiing. From then on it was an annual family trip for the Christmas holidays and, after three years, we added Easter week. But it was tough for my dad to budget the money and the time to drive. We couldn't afford to fly,

WARRENISM

"If scientists are so smart, why haven't they discovered a disease that can be cured by skiing and snowboarding."

because he was putting all his money back into the manufacturing plant where he was making automobile radiators. One Easter week, he didn't even get to go with the family because he was having union problems and had to stay home to resolve them. By that time, we were all hooked on skiing. Mom did almost all of the driving except when she got sleepy. I did some of it across Iowa and eastern Colorado when we thought the police weren't around.

"That Easter I was 14 years old, and I got to be pals with the ski patrol. When we got home I studied for my first-aid certificate. The next year I started helping out by volunteering to work part-time as a ski patrolman during Christmas and Easter week. By the time I was in college, I was spending more time skiing in Colorado than I was with my college studies.

"I managed to study enough between ski trips, and I got my engineering degree three years ago. Then I started to work full-time for my dad. My dad always told me that someday I would run and then own the radiator manufacturing business that his father had started 60 years earlier.

"Then it happened. I came back into the plant after a Christmas holiday of powder-snow skiing, full-moon nights, meeting and skiing with wonderful people, and enjoying great dinner parties. And as I wandered around the radiator shop and heard the noisy din of manufacturing, I thought, 'Is this where I want to spend the rest of my life?'

"That same day I took my dad to lunch and said, 'Pop, I can't do it. I'm going out to Colorado, and I'll be a ski patrolman for a year or two. I can work construction during the summer, because I just don't want to spend my life running a factory in Detroit. I'm sorry.'

"He knew arguing was useless, and with a tear in his eye, my dad said, 'If only I hadn't taken you to so many Warren Miller films, then maybe I could be moving out to Colorado instead of you. I really hate that Warren Miller.'"

The lift ride was almost over when the Vail patroller asked, "D'ya mind if I ski down behind you?" As we pushed off into perfect powder snow, with the blue sky overhead and the Gore Range shimmering in the distance, he added: "By the way, Warren, thanks a lot for messing up my life."

STRANGE BUT TRUE

Science Comes to Skiing

It was a cold spring day in 1935 at the summit of the Weissfluggipfel in Davos, Switzerland. Forty-three ski racers were ready to put their lives on the line in a 12-kilometer downhill race to the village of Kublis.

This would be the toughest downhill ever held. A racer could take any route to the bottom and the only control gate was their courage. With enough courage and ability, a racer could take all the shortcuts he could find. He could cut through farms, down icy, manure-covered paths, and, if the snow was deep enough, ski right over fences. (One of the better racers had been overheard bribing a farmer and his wife to take down part of their fence on the day of the race so his line from top to bottom could be even shorter and faster.) During training, the farmers learned what happens when a hurtling body collides with a cow, a sheep or a goat. Even the chickens began to get crazy as the racers practiced their many different shortcuts through the farmyards at the then unheard-of speed of more than 25 miles per hour.

On race day, curious spectators queued up early to ride the new-fangled Parsenn Bahn cable railway to watch the anticipated carnage. The forerunner shoved off to the shouts of encouragement from several dozen spectators. He had a large, clanging Swiss cowbell tied around his neck to warn people and animals to get out of the way. Not one of the best skiers, he fell innumerable times on his 12-kilometer journey and finally arrived in Kublis some 34 minutes later, dirty, sweaty, bleeding and completely exhausted. Upon his arrival, race officials waved a special flag at the telegraph operator at the nearby railroad station to telephone Davos Dorf, to telephone the Weissflujoch station at the top of the Parsenn Bahn, to raise another special flag so the race officials at the top of the course

would know the course was clear and ready for the racers.

The first racer across the finish line wore bib number three. Dirty and disheveled, his racing bib torn almost off his body, he reported that a farmer had forgotten about the race and walked his cows home after their morning watering, leaving their droppings in the middle of his route.

Then, one by one, the racers struggled and straggled in with their various tales of near-death experiences at speeds never before thought possibe. One racer, finishing with a broken nose and blood all over his face, reported that his shortcut to a barnyard was suddenly blocked by a string of cows. Without metal edges on his skis, he couldn't turn on the ice in the shade of the barn, so at the last second he lay down on the backs of his skis and slid right under one cow.

As the racers straggled in, their times continued to drop until bib number 19 came in with a time under 25 minutes. The crowd went berserk. Then a young Swiss racer came hurtling out of the trees from a completely different direction, heading for the finish line with a bib number that was completely out of sequence. Either he had started at the wrong time, or he had passed a dozen racers on the way down. His was the fastest time of the day—by almost 10 minutes!

His name was Walter Prager, and he would later become the most famous ski coach in Dartmouth College history. That day he set a record for the Parsenn Derby downhill that would stand for over a decade.

Walter was one of the few racers that day with metal edges on his skis. Metal edges were a recent invention; many racers had not even seen them before, and some of those who had considered them too dangerous to have so close to their body when they fell.

Walter had spent a week before the race diagramming all of the different routes. He came to the conclusion that all of his left turns would be on ice or hard-packed snow and all of his right turns would be on soft corn snow. So the night before the race he unscrewed all the interlocking pieces of the steel edges on the right side of his skis and replaced them with his own handmade brass edges. His uncle, an engineer and a skier, too, had convinced him that brass edges would have a lower coefficient of friction in the warmer temperature range of the corn snow.

And that's how science first entered the world of skiing.

Monkeying Around On Skis

In the 1930s, any hill with a ropetow was called a ski resort. Never mind that it had a small and always muddy parking lot and that the ropetow always stopped while you were hanging onto it. It was still called a ski resort.

So if a ropetow was a ski resort, then there used to be a ski resort where Universal Studios stands today in North Hollywood.

On a fairly flat hill with a view of the San Fernando Valley and all of the orange trees, Austrian ski instructor Sepp Benedikter hung the upper sheave wheel of a ropetow from an oak tree. The power to run the rope came from the jacked-up back wheel of his Model A Ford. In place of snow, he and some of his friends had hauled a couple of truckloads of pine needles down from the San Bernadino Mountains and spread them around with rakes.

It was on that hill that I first witnessed someone making a turn on a pair of skis.

I had ridden my bicycle from where I lived in Hollywood up over Cahuenga Pass into the San Fernando Valley. I was headed for a new tourist attraction that I had read about: Monkey Island! It was near the first valley stop on the Pacific Electric Railroad, the route of "The Big Red Cars." Admission to Monkey Island was 10 cents.

An investor had built a 40-foot-high fake plaster and cement mountain and surrounded it with a 20-foot-wide moat of slimy green, stagnant water. You paid your 10 cents and got to watch about a hundred under-nourished monkeys sitting on the concrete mountain sullenly watching you watching them. For another five cents you could buy a bag of peanuts to throw at the monkeys. If the peanuts fell into the water, the more adventuresome monkeys would wade out and pick

Austrian ski instructor Sepp Benedikter sailed over the pine-needle ski slope where Universal Studios and the Sheraton Universal Hotel now stand.

them up one by one. I was told later by the combination ticket seller, ticket taker, peanut salesman, monkey keeper and owner that the monkeys had recently been disappearing one by one. He had finally figured out that they had learned to swim across the moat at night to escape the concrete island. His suspicions had been confirmed just the day before when an alert newspaper photographer had snapped a picture of a monkey in an orange tree about half a mile away.

As I gazed across Monkey Island and tried unsuccessfully to understand all of the potential ramifications of such a moneymaking tourist attraction, I could see movement on a hill about half a mile away. It looked as though a half-dozen bent-over people were sliding up and down the ridge below the solitary oak tree.

By then I was tired of the morose monkeys staring at me staring at them, so I climbed on my blue bicycle and pedaled over to see what was going on at the lone oak tree on the green hill. What I found was a ski resort. It was so hot that day that several of the skiers were making turns without shirts. I laid my bicycle down on the grass and walked partway up the hill to watch the skiers making turns on pine needles and squashed green grass that was turning various shades of yellow and brown.

For the first time in my life I heard words spoken in German, words like *stembogen*, *vorlage* and *sitzmark*, to mention just a few.

The ski slope could not have been longer than a couple of hundred feet, but I was awestruck by the concept. The skiers were free to go wherever their skis wanted to take them. For a better view I climbed to the top of the hill and sat down under the oak tree. To the northeast I could see row upon endless row of orange trees, clear across the San Fernando Valley. I was really excited about being a spectator to such an unbelievable sight—the only spectator, I might add.

About the time I was absorbing all of these new sights, the remains of an acorn landed right in front of me. Then another and another. Looking up I saw three of the escapees from Monkey Island. They had found an ample supply of acorns to live on and enough crazy skiers to watch to keep them completely amused.

The next weekend I brought a friend on a bicycle trip over Cahuenga Pass to see Monkey Island and the Oak Tree Ski Resort. There was a closed sign on the entrance to the tourist attraction, the water had been drained out of the moat, the monkeys were all gone...and so was the ropetow. Sepp Benedikter, his ropetow and his band of hardy skiers had moved to a sand dune near 34th Street in Manhattan Beach for the rest of the summer.

My Second Day on Skis

I sat on the curb waiting for my ride. Each time I exhaled, my breath was a misty cloud backlit by the glare of the streetlight half a block away. It was already 4 a.m., and I was wondering why my ride hadn't showed up yet. Overhead, a million stars were shimmering on this very cold January morning in 1937.

This was to be a genuine Boy Scout ski trip to Mt. San Jacinto, high above Palm Springs. My $2 pine skis and bamboo poles lay in the wet grass alongside my canvas rucksack. In my rucksack were four peanut butter, jam and oleomargarine sandwiches, four fig bars, and an apple. I was wearing my almost-knee-high hiking boots with the pocket on the outside of the right boot that held my pocketknife. I never went hiking without a pocketknife in case a rattlesnake bit me. (I didn't know what I'd do if I got bitten, but at least I had the right kind of knife, just in case.) My wool socks with red stripes around the tops were turned down over the tops of the boots, and I had a plaid wool shirt on over my sweatshirt.

This was actually my second trip to the snow. On my first ski trip I had frozen my buns. Born and raised in Southern California, I had had no cold-weather experience—I had never even heard of long underwear. So this time I was wisely wearing my cotton pajamas under my Sears and Roebuck Levis and carrying the gear I'd bought in the one Army surplus store left in Los Angeles. Even in those days Army surplus stores had creaky wooden floors and barrels of all kinds of stuff you just couldn't do without. I had parted with 25 cents of my hard-earned money for a black wool hat and 10 cents for a pair of cotton gloves that I later soaked in melted paraffin to make them really waterproof.

Now, as I waited for my ride, adrenaline was keeping me warm.

WARREN MILLER '02

Just as the cold began to creep into my skinny teenage body, a pair of headlights turned the corner and headed down my dark street.

I was the last one to be picked up, joining David, Bill, Jim, George and Johnny. Johnny was the rich one in the group; he had his own four-door sedan. The rest of us had agreed to kick in 30 cents each for our share of the gas for the three-hour trip. Johnny's big black 1935 Chevrolet had wide running boards, straight sides, a flat roof and windows that rolled down. It also had a spare tire mounted on the back. Because ski racks hadn't been invented yet, we wrapped our skis and poles in a blanket and then stuffed them between the tire and the back of the car and tied them down.

Only three of us had skis and poles. David, Bill and George had come along for the ride and the hike up to the snow. I didn't know it, but they were planning on taking turns with my pine skis and bamboo poles when I got tired.

Two hours later, as we were leaving the small town of Hemet and beginning the long climb up the winding road to Mt. San Jacinto, the stars began to fade, and the clear black sky began to turn gray. Across the valley to the east, 10,000-foot Mt. San Gorgonio was beginning to take shape, the top of it covered in snow.

Finally, four hours after we left my house in Hollywood, we parked at the trailhead. There, just as people have been doing since skis and automobiles were invented, we untied our skis and leaned them against the side of the car. They promptly fell over and scratched the right front fender.

Rather than carry a heavy lunch in my rucksack, I decided to eat a sandwich or two before I started hiking. Then I put on my rucksack and, just as I had seen on a poster somewhere, slung my skis over my right shoulder. We began the long climb up to where we hoped there would be snow from the last storm.

Johnny immediately started singing, and we all joined in a robust yet slightly altered version of "When Johnny Comes Marching Home Again, Hurrah, Hurrah!" The Boy Scout chorale lasted about 20 yards and then we gave it up and concentrated on gasping for breath.

The decomposed granite of this ancient mountain crunched under our feet, and the screech of blue jays replaced the screech of sea gulls that we were used to. To me, this was what belonging to the Boy Scouts was all about: exploration, discovery, adventure and being out of breath.

After about two hours of climbing, resting and climbing, we found a patch of snow that was wide enough and deep enough to handle five or six turns (except none of us could do that many turns without falling). It was about 30 feet wide, 100 feet long and six inches deep. It was also hard and crusty from constant melting and freezing.

Today we would call it corn snow.

Johnny had a pair of ridgetop skis with metal edges, metal Kandahar bindings, real ski boots with box toes and varnished split-bamboo ski poles. He also had a copy of Otto Lang's 1935 ski instruction book that cost $1.25 that he pulled out of his rucksack. Before we put on our skis, we sat on a rock at the top of this virgin snowfield and turned the pages until we got to the good stuff: how to make a snow-plow turn.

With my $2 pine skis without edges and my toe-strap bindings, I practiced traversing across the melting snow. By dragging my poles more and more aggressively, I managed to occasionally come to a stop before I skied off the edge of the snowfield and onto the dirt, where I always fell. There I would pick myself up, step out of my skis, pick them up, point them back in the other direction and begin to traverse again. But before I could move I had to slide them back and forth on the snow to get the mud off the bottoms.

Johnny was a hot skier. He had gone to Yosemite with his family for the Christmas holidays. He had actually stayed in a hotel and eaten in restaurants and ridden on the boat tow at Badger Pass. He had been taught how to ski by Hannes Schroll and Sigi Engl. Now he could actually make linked snowplow turns down the face of that flat snowfield. After watching him for a while, I knew it was time for me to try a snowplow turn. As I attempted to turn that first time, absolutely nothing happened. My heels went apart and my toes were pointing at each other, but my skis were still going straight. Several more attempts later I heard the splintering of wood as the toe strap pulled the top of my left ski right off.

Skiing on San Jacinto that day was over for me.

An hour and a half later Johnny finally got tired and quit, so we all

"Skiing is what happens when you change your plans."

got our gear together and headed back down to the car. I carried the remains of one of my $2 skis in my rucksack and the other ski over my shoulder. I knew I could glue the broken parts back together in my junior high school wood shop class.

At the car we were greeted by a flat tire and a spare with no air in it. We jacked up the car and, with tire irons, got the tire off the rim and pulled out the inner tube. We pumped up the tube and then drew straws to see who would hike down to the creek and sink the tube in water to locate the leak by looking for escaping bubbles.

When Bill returned from the creek with the leaking inner tube, we sandpapered around the hole, applied glue to the tube and to a patch, then clamped tube and patch together for a few minutes. Finally we reinserted the tube into the tire, manhandled the tire onto the rim with the tire irons, and pumped the tire up with a hand pump until it was firm enough to drive on.

It was already dark as we got underway. As Johnny wheeled the black Chevrolet down the winding mountain road, we could see the lights of Hemet far below and San Bernadino off in the distance.

Before we had driven three miles I was sound asleep. How long I slept I don't know, but I woke up to the squeal of tires. The car was leaning precariously to the right, and then we were upside down and flying, crashing, bouncing and rolling amid the grinding of metal and the crashing of glass.

When the noise and frightening motion were over, I crawled around in broken glass on the ceiling of the car, wiggled out through a broken window and fell in a heap in a ditch alongside the upside down car.

All the boys were shouting back and forth: "Are you O.K.?" I didn't answer. It was obvious to me that my arm was badly broken and my wrist dislocated. My Boy Scout training took over, and I wouldn't let anyone move me until medical help arrived. The first help that showed up was the local veterinarian on his way home from delivering lambs at a nearby farm. It only took him a couple of minutes to figure out the extent of my injuries.

"No problem," he said. "One of you hold his upper arm. I'll just pull his hand out a little and the dislocated wrist will snap back into place. The broken bone should be fine. I'll just squeeze it back into position and splint it. When you get him back home, he can get an X-ray if he wants to. There shouldn't be any problem."

When that veterinarian pulled on my hand to straighten out my broken arm and dislocated wrist, it felt like he had stretched it out to where it was about 11 feet long. When he let go of it, I passed out from the pain. Next thing I knew the others had somehow turned the car right side up and decided that it was in good enough shape to drive back to Los Angeles. I climbed into the back seat and tried to get comfortable. The shock of the accident kept the pain from bothering me too much. I even managed to doze off a few times. All I could think of was, "I wonder if my arm will be well before all the snow melts."

We arrived back at my house just before midnight. It was completely dark. In my condition, I thought I could sneak upstairs and into bed without waking anyone up.

No such luck.

As I climbed up onto the porch, I dropped what was left of my skis. Lights instantly went on all over the house. The front door opened, and there stood my mother. As I started through the door, the narrow escape and everything else finally got to me and I projectile vomited all over my mother and the living room rug.

I knew better days on skis still lay ahead.

A Shortcut to Fame

I n 1939, a narrow, dusty dirt road led north from the small, until recently almost abandoned mining town of Ketchum, Idaho. About two miles west of town, an even narrower winding ski trail had been cut the summer before from the top of 9,000-foot Bald Mountain, which the locals simply called Baldy. Where the trail met the valley floor, hot sulphur springs flowed into the Big Wood River. Here and there was a natural pool you could soak your tired body in, even during the below-zero days of January.

The narrow, winding trail was to be the site of the first Harriman Cup downhill ski race, named after Averell Harriman, the visionary who founded Sun Valley. It was the toughest downhill race that America had to offer. Partway down the winding, narrow trail, there was an awesome steilhang. At the bottom there was a wicked transition and left turn that would give any skier with enough courage more speed than his equipment or his body could handle.

The racers used stiff, hickory, ridge-top skis, seven-feet-six-inches long without plastic bottoms or offset edges. They had bindings that wouldn't release in any direction no matter how they fell. When they fell, their body would sometimes revolve a time or two more than their legs would.

Halfway down the trail, the race course designer, Friedl Pfeiffer, had cut seven turns that were very narrow and twisting because the hill was so steep. Each one required a very sharp turn to miss the trees on either side, turns that the better racers tried to straighten out as much as possible so they could go faster. As they did, they came danger-ously close to the trees on either side of the trail.

The pre-race favorite was a young man named Dick Durrance,

who had placed eighth at the 1936 Olympics in Germany. In the days leading up to the race, Dick kept looking for a faster, straighter line through those seven dangerous turns. The trees between the turns were so close together that taking a shortcut through them looked impossible. The turns were so sharp that the race committee felt that no control gates were necessary there.

With the skill born of a half-dozen years of racing experience, Dick spent a lot of time sighting through the trees, looking at them every which way until he finally had it figured out. If just one small tree were cut down and removed, he figured, he could straighten out all seven turns and save an enormous amount of time.

Why not?

Late in the afternoon on the day before the race, Dick climbed up Warm Springs with a saw, a shovel and a friend; together they sawed down that one tree that stood in the way of Dick's secret shortcut. Once they had dragged the tree out of the way, they returned to cover their tracks and the scattered pine needles with snow.

Now all that remained for Dick to do was climb back up the course and decide where he could get lined up for his straight shot through the seven turns. He decided not to practice the shortcut for fear that someone else might see his tracks and try it, too.

Now that he had his line figured out, Dick and his fellow conspirator found another smaller tree, sawed it down and carried it over to where the first tree had been cut down. There they propped it upright in the same place as the original tree.

Their plan was set. On race day, as soon as it was determined which racing number Dick would have, his partner, lurking in the woods, would simply count the racers as they went by and then yank the substitute tree out of the way so Dick could take his shortcut. Once Dick raced by, his partner would reinsert the tree so no on else could take the straighter line.

Everything worked perfectly. Racers one through three roared by, making slow, wide arcs around all seven turns. Then it was time to yank the tree. Dick took his shortcut, and his partner immediately reinserted the substitute tree.

But Dick forgot one thing: He came out of his shortcut at such a high rate of speed that he missed the final turn at the bottom of the course, a right turn to the finish line.

Instead, he skidded on and on until he wound up splashing knee-deep into the Big Wood River. Still, he managed to clamber out of the ice-cold water, climb up to the finish line and fall across it to win the race by two full seconds.

And that's how Dick Durrance became the first winner of the Harriman Cup and also ended up riding back to the Sun Valley Lodge that day in wet clothes and boots.

Three days later he was fined $2 by the Forest Service for chopping down a tree on government property without a permit.

Chairlift Lines

The chairlift on Ruud Mountain at Sun Valley in 1947 had one very peculiar characteristic. If you didn't sit down gently when you started your ride, the cable would start bouncing a little bit, and through some unique mathematical equation of time versus distance, a rare harmonic vibration would be set up. Your small initial bounce would be rapidly magnified until, just before you got to the first tower, you would be thrown unceremoniously out of the chair, landing in the snow 10 feet below. (This would only happen in front of your friends, of course.) Even after you learned of the lift's idiosyncrasy, trying to hang on each time you made a mistake getting on was nearly impossible. This was, after all, only the second or third chairlift built in the world, and 1937 engineering knowledge wasn't all that sophisticated.

Until 1936, when the first chairlift was invented, one of the few ways you could get a real thrill out of skiing was to be a Nordic ski jumper. For each jump, you would have to spend at least half an hour climbing up to the top of the hill, or in-run, with your thick, wide, heavy eight-foot skis over your shoulder. At the top you'd rest a bit, put your skis on, and then start down the in-run, gaining as much speed as the hill allowed until you flew, or jumped, off the lip. Depending on the height of the hill, the object was always to go far enough through the air as possible to come in for a gentle landing at the tangent to the steep landing hill.

Nordic jumping was most popular in the Midwest, where the hills are not very high. At most locations, ski clubs would spend every summer weekend building a scaffold for their new, bigger, higher in-run, way above the top of the landing hill. The agony of climbing, the shakiness of

Union Pacific engineers tested a mock-up of the world's first chairlift in the company's railroad yard in Omaha in the summer of 1936.

the scaffolds built out of scrounged lumber and the lack of safety bindings kept most people from ever becoming ski jumpers, and thus, skiers.

This began to change in 1936, when the chairlift was invented by a Union Pacific Railroad engineer. Skiing immediately began to come of age because, at the same time, the railroad also invented Sun Valley, Idaho. Now, you could finally ski downhill all day long and never have to climb back up. Just sit down in a moving chair and be hauled back up for as many rides as your strength, skill and money allowed. And all of this for only a couple of dollars a day for a ski lift ticket.

When it was decided to build Sun Valley, one of the first memos written by W. Averell Harriman, president of the railroad, called for "mechanical devices to take people to the tops of the slides." Engineers in Omaha, Nebraska, home base of the railroad, immediately went to work on variations of the already invented ropetow (1934) and the J-Bar (1935).

A young railroad engineer named Jim Curran, who had helped build equipment for loading bananas on fruit boats in the tropics, was a member of the railroad team assigned to the task. To him, transporting skiers or bunches of bananas without bruising them presented much the same problem. The only difference was the temperature in which they were transported. All Curran did was replace the banana hooks that hung from a moving cable with chairs for people to sit on.

His original drawings were almost overlooked in the first presentation to Averell Harriman; but former Olympic skier, Dartmouth ski coach and consultant Charlie Proctor spotted the drawings and sent them on to Harriman with his recommendations.

"Curran's ideas are the best. Let him design and build the whole thing!"

By July, a mock-up of the chair was built in the bed of a pickup truck in a hot railroad yard in Omaha, Nebraska. A bunch of timbers resembling half of a T were hung out over the side of the truck. Hanging from this structure was a free swinging, two-inch-in-diameter piece of pipe. The chair seat was welded to the bottom of the pipe and was the same distance off the ground as a normal chair with legs. Jim Curran's engineering team thought that they could drive the pickup truck with the chair facing forward and scoop up the waiting-in-line skier. Driving the truck at various speeds, they could eventually decide on which speed was the best, and fastest, to scoop up waiting skiers without injuring them. Time was running out. They had less than five months left to invent, design, engineer, build, test and begin hauling paying passengers up the side of a hill in the remote wilds of Idaho by Christmas. A decision on final design had to be made quickly, so expert skier John E.P. Morgan was summoned to Omaha to test this revolutionary new idea. He arrived with skis, boots, poles and wearing woolen ski clothes. He looked, and had to feel, pretty silly standing around sweating amid the steam engines and a handful of railroad engineers involved in a top-secret project. At first, Morgan simply stood on a pile of straw as the truck drove up slowly and tried to scoop him up. Straw proved not to be slippery enough, and Morgan picked himself up from the cinder-covered railroad yard a few dozen times.

At lunch someone suggested, "Why not add some oil to the straw?"

They did, and now John had oily straw stuck to the bottom of his skis. That didn't slide very well either.

Then a junior engineer suggested, "Let's try a pair of roller skates. There's some concrete out by the roundhouse that we can drive back and forth on."

A couple of hours later, with Morgan sweating profusely in his thick woolen ski clothes and roller skates, the maximum speed for loading live bodies on a chairlift was decided—a speed, incidentally, that is still being used in fixed-grip chairlifts all over the world today.

The engineers now started working around the clock until all of the working drawings were completed. Construction on the various parts was begun in the railroad machine shop as fast as they were designed. Most of them were built railroad-strong in those Omaha shops. While this was progressing, some of the engineering crew rode the train out to Sun Valley to get "The Tramway" under construction. The purpose, as the *Hailey Weekly* newspaper said, was "to carry ski jumpers up to where they will shoot back down."

The lift towers on that world's first chairlift were single wooden poles that could easily double for telephone poles. On top of the poles the cross pieces that supported the wheels, or sheaves, that the cable ran over were made of metal. Because the sheaves were metal, every time the grip that attached the chair to the cable bumped over them, your chair got a real jolt.

Fortunately, it wasn't a double chairlift, because the ride was so noisy that you never could have heard anything your partner was saying anyway.

In the summer of 1936 there was no such thing as a tractor that could climb Dollar Mountain to haul all of the materials up to erect the new Tramway. The parts were hauled up by pack mule or on the backs of 10-cents-an-hour, out-of-work miners.

While the lift was under construction, Sun Valley's publicity genius, Steve Hannigan, gave this remote Idaho Tramway a new name that is as famous today as the sport itself. Hannigan coined the name "chairlift."

It was completed on time, on budget, for the grand Christmas opening. However, there was no reason for anyone to ride it until after the arrival of the first snowfall, which didn't show up until January ninth. Once the snow arrived in the valley, the Dollar lift started running without a problem.

It had been made railroad-strong.

My first experience with that "first in the world ski lift," according to my diary, was on January 27, 1947, when a very attractive young lady invited me for lunch at the Dollar Mountain Cabin. I didn't know it when I accepted the date, but the cabin was at the top of the lift. I didn't want to miss my luncheon date, but I couldn't afford a $4 lift ticket to get up there. (I had already figured out the Baldy lift operator manipulation system so I could ride those lifts without a ticket.) So I did the next best thing: I arrived at the base of Dollar an hour early, climbed to the top of the mountain and skied over to the sun porch of the Dollar Cabin. I enjoyed the great lunch and my date's Texas accent. After lunch, Josephine Abercrombie and her girlfriend, Audrey Beck, seemed to be content to just lean back and soak up the sun, so I took a calculated risk. I climbed into my skis, waved good-bye for awhile, and skied down the west ridge of the Dollar Bowl in beautiful, untracked powder snow. At the bottom, I skied right up to get back on the lift as though I had been riding it all day.

"Can I see your lift ticket please?"

"OH! I left it on my parka. It's hanging up on the sun deck at the restaurant at the top."

"Be sure to bring it down next time."

"Sure, I will."

I didn't have a parka, so I looked around the sun deck at the top, spotted one with a lift ticket hanging on it, found out who owned it, and said to the owner, "I'm really cold; could I borrow your parka and make a few runs wearing it?"

The guy who loaned it to me was busy trying to hustle my date and sipping Dom Perignon while soaking up the sun's warm rays alongside the two ladies from Texas. I skied four of five runs with that borrowed lift ticket. Each time at the bottom of the lift, I chatted for a few minutes with the lift operator about his old days on the railroad, his farm in Hailey, how his herd of cows was doing, how early he had to get up to milk all of them to be here in time to start the lift, how many kids he had, where he was born, how hard he worked, important stuff like that.

By the fifth run, that lift operator invited me down to have dinner at this farmhouse some night soon. By this time he knew me so well he never asked to see my lift ticket again for the rest of the winter. At the top, on the fifth run, I gave the parka back to the man I had borrowed it from and skied free the rest of the day with Josephine and Audrey.

I was virtually guaranteed free lift rides when, a week or so later, I had dinner at the lift operator's farmhouse and met his incredibly beautiful daughter. He told me that he really appreciated it when I didn't make a pass at her. The retired railroad engineer, now Hailey farmer and lift operator, said, "Warren, as long as I'm taking tickets, you can ski free on Dollar for the rest of the winter."

More ski lift history.

In 1948, Sun Valley management decided to build a new chairlift up the ridge between the two Dollar Bowls in order to open up more ski terrain. How word of tearing down old ski lifts spreads I don't know. Even in 1948 there wasn't much of a market for a 12-year-old chairlift. However, a man who would later design, build and own the best ski resort in the Midwest heard about it being for sale. Driving out from Boyne Mountain, Michigan, in a flatbed truck, Everett Kircher brought with him his new ski school director, Victor Gottchaulk.

It took Everett a couple of days to negotiate the final price of the lift with Pappy Rogers, the general manager of Sun Valley. Pappy had a price in his mind that Everett thought was unconscionable. Pappy wanted $5,200 for the lift, as is, but Everett finally beat him down to $4,800.

As soon as Everett's check cleared the bank, Pappy Rogers let him get to work. He and Victor got busy with their spanner wrenches and spent the next two weeks dismantling the world's first chairlift. Piece by piece, the two of them loaded it onto their truck and hauled it down to the Ketchum railroad siding, where they loaded it onto a flatbed railroad car. They then climbed into their truck with a full load of stuff and drove back to Boyne Mountain, Michigan. The bull wheels, the large wheels at the top and bottom of the chairlift that allow the cable to change direction, turned out to be very large in diameter. While driving their truck back to Michigan, Everett and Victor mentally redesigned their old single chairlift into a double. The bull wheels were large enough in diameter to keep the cable far enough away from the lift towers so the chairs could carry two people at a time. They even added a new, radical design of rubber-tired sheaves on the towers so the ride up would be quieter. What I liked most about the rubber-tired wheel was that you didn't bounce every time you went over every tower. Everett coverted that single chair to a double chair two years later.

A few years ago, when I last rode that old Number One lift at Boyne Mountain, Michigan, the upper and lower bull wheels and the original gears from the engine that drove the lower bull wheel shaft in 1936, were still carrying skiers "to where they will shoot back down." That's over 50 years after it was invented in Omaha, Nebraska, by a group of engineers who had never skied a day in their lives.

They built that lift railroad-strong, and the basic design of that first chairlift has worked perfectly since it first scooped up E.P. Morgan, on his roller skates, on a hot July afternoon in Omaha in 1936.

A Day of Skiing for $1.75

The other day I received the annual fall issues of the ski magazines, plus the other catalogs of ski equipment and merchandise that arrive at my house every year before Labor Day. These publications rank the top 60 resorts in America, tell you what skis are hot, list the latest prices for ski country condos and land, and contain hundreds of pages of four-color advertising telling you why last year's high-tech gear is no longer usable.

By the time I had thumbed halfway through all this, I was sound asleep.

Here are some quotes from a ski resort brochure dated 1940.

Ski Time Is Thrill Time

"Just to be in the skiing country in the winter is a wonderful experience in itself. You come out on a bright morning, take deep stimulating breaths of the winey air and look about you on a White-Christmas-like world more entrancing than anything you have ever seen before. And then you're off on the trail or 'schussing' your skis down a fast slope...great!

"Try it yourself. It's easy...surprisingly easy. That's why the number of skiers had doubled every year in recent years. You don't have to be any special age to enjoy the sport. Enough can be learned in a short time to enable you to do cross-country skiing and simple downhill coasting that will bring real thrills.

"There are other sports at the ski resorts, too. Skating, tobogganing, bob sledding, snowshoeing, skijoring, cutter riding and dog-sled mushing...all offering a world of excitement and fun. Dancing and other evening entertainment round out the day of fun and frolic."

Now let's look at the fine print that the many ski resorts in the

ski-time is thrill time!

in WISCONSIN—Upper MICHIGAN—SUN VALLEY, IDAHO

LAKE GENEVA AND WILLIAMS BAY

ski-time

1-Day Trip $1 75 = From CHICAGO

Sundays and Holidays, December 24 to March 31
(Not including February 12)

Here's enjoyment and excitement for Chicagoland winter sports fans within the reach of all! Board a North Western SKI-TIME train on Sunday or Holiday mornings and be off to a glorious day of fun and thrills at either Lake Geneva or Williams Bay—just a short run by train.

Good skiing on the hills bordering the lake. Also skating and ice boating. At Williams Bay is a good toboggan run with warm shelter house serving hot lunches at low cost.

All winter sports activities both at Lake Geneva and Williams Bay are close to C. & N. W. station.

Return to Chicago in the late afternoon the same day.

No meals on trains or at destination included.

C. & N. W. Ry. Train Schedules

GOING:		RETURNING:	
Lv. Chicago	7.55 am	Lv. Williams Bay	4.40 pm
Lv. Clybourn	8.02 am	Lv. Lake Geneva	4.50 pm
Lv. Irving Park	8.07 am	Ar. Jefferson Park	6.22 pm
Lv. Jefferson Park	8.12 am	Ar. Clybourn	6.33 pm
Ar. Lake Geneva	10.15 am	Ar. Chicago	6.40 pm
Ar. Williams Bay	10.25 am		

(#) On Dec. 25, Jan. 1 and Feb. 22 this rate will be $2.60 to Lake Geneva and $2.80 to William. Bay.

WILLIAMS BAY, WISCONSIN

Season: December 22 to March 31

$4 00 and up from CHICAGO

THE GENEVA LAKE area has some of the best skiing hills in the whole southern Wisconsin-northern Illinois region within easy walking distance of the resorts at Williams Bay. Well kept skating rinks. Exciting toboggan runs. Ice boating on the lake.

THE ROSE LANE RESORT
HOTEL NORMANDIE

All are comfortable lodging resorts within easy walking distance of the winter sports area. Meals can be obtained at several good places—Spence's Dining Room and Lee's Kitchen.

"SKI-TIME" Week-End Trip Costs Per Person
From CHICAGO

(Leave Saturday and return Sunday evening, also leave on Sunday and return Monday at costs shown below; and on Tuesday, Feb. 21 and return Wednesday, Feb. 22 at $1.05 higher than costs shown below.)

Train Accommodations	Train Schedules J	A and E shown below	B and E shown below	C and E shown below	D and E shown below
In Coaches....		$4.25	$4.25	$4.15	$4.00

Above prices also include transfers between depot and resorts, and
Lodgings—2 to a room with bathing facilities (25c extra per night for single room.)
Additional Days—For those desiring to leave earlier and stay longer add $1.75 per person for each additional day—2 to a room with bathing facilities; $2.00 for single room.
No meals on trains or at destination included.

C. & N. W. Train Schedules

GOING:	"A"	"B"	"C"	"D"	RETURNING:	"E"	
	am	am	pm	pm		pm	pm
Lv. Chicago	f 8.19	g 7.55	h 2.00	j 5.18	Lv. Williams Bay	g 4.40	f 1.35
Ar. Williams Bay	11.10	10.25	3.45	7.03	Ar. Chicago	6.40	4.10

f—Daily except Sundays and Holidays.   h—Saturdays only.
g—Sundays and Holidays only.   j—Daily except Saturdays, Sundays and Holidays.

1940 brochure have to offer.

Lake Geneva and Williams Bay, Wisconsin

"Here's enjoyment and excitement for Chicago-land winter sports fans within reach of all. Board a Northwestern ski-time train on a Sunday or holiday morning and be off for a glorious day of fun and thrills at either Lake Geneva or Williams Bay...Just a short run by train.

"Good skiing on the hills bordering the lake. Also skating and ice boating. At Williams Bay is a good toboggan run with a warm shelter house serving hot lunches at low cost."

The cost?

Round trip train fromChicago is $1.75.

That's right.

One dollar and seventy-five cents for a fun-filled day of skiing, and that includes transportation to the resort and return to Chicago.

In 1940, the people who could find a job were earning 25 cents an hour. A Coca Cola was five cents. A hamburger was 10 cents, a milk-shake was also a dime, and it cost 25 cents to see a first-run movie. I was earning $3 a week delivering morning newspapers, and that $12 a month was enough to buy my school clothes and gas for a $25 car so I could get to the beach and go surfing every weekend. In 1940 there were only six chairlifts in the United States.

Wausau, Wisconsin

"Just a short distance outside of Wausau, with an open slope 400 feet wide and 2,500 feet long, with six trails varying in speed and diffi-culty, offers a place for both the beginner and the professional to improve their skills and enjoy themselves to the fullest. A 3,150-foot ski tow—A SKIER'S DELIGHT—takes all of the work out of skiing and doubles the number of down slope rides you can get in one day."

Because the ski lift was 650 feet longer than the hill, I assume it ran clear downtown to the railroad station.

Prices start at $8.15 round trip from Chicago and $6.40 from Milwaukee.

Gasoline had already gone up in price by 1940 and cost as much as 13 cents a gallon.

Sun Valley, Idaho

Imagine if you can a large valley sheltered by rugged mountains all covered with a deep blanket of dry powder snow sparkling in the brilliant sun. There you have Sun Valley, America's foremost winter sports center.

The heavy snows last until late spring. CHAIR SKI LIFTS and snow tractors available to Sun Valley guests pack more skiing thrills into a few hours at Sun Valley than any other place in the world.

Prices start at $88.35 all expenses from Chicago and return. This includes the transfer from the train in Ketchum to Sun Valley, all meals on the train and at Sun Valley, as well as ski lift tickets. This is for a seven and a half day trip, and if you want to stay extra days they start at $6.75 for three meals, your room and ski lift ticket.

At ski resorts today, $6.75 might get you a lukewarm cappuccino from a waiter who has to commute 29 miles from his 18-foot house trailer. That same waiter will have a second job teaching skiing so he can afford to spend his just-out-of-college formative years at a ski resort.

I am very lucky.

I was able to enjoy those inexpensive days of skiing. Of course, I'm also lucky because I can still enjoy them today, probably a lot more because of grooming, snowmaking, quad chairlifts, warm clothes, fat skis and safety bindings.

At higher prices, of course.

But then how much do skiers earn in one hour today? Fifty times the 25 cents an hour we earned in 1940? Or is it 100 times that amount?

It's all relative.

Skiing is still a bargain. It's all the other things you do on a ski trip that cost all the money, like eating, sleeping and buying T-shirts.

Lifts Long Forgotten

T he ski scene in California was always unique, even in the late 1930s when I started skiing. For one thing, T-shirts were the costume of choice in the Southern California mountains. Carloads of people would leave the 80-degree springtime heat of Fullerton or Anaheim and drive up to the San Bernadino mountains to throw snowballs at each other—or at passing cars. They wore T-shirts. Skiers dressed the same way.

On Mt. Baldy, a T-shirt wasn't always the best costume for ascending the mountain. The resort had an access lift that rose about 1,500 vertical feet up to The Notch, so named because it was the wind tunnel of the San Bernadinos. By the time Mom, Dad and their two kids got to the top of the lift, they would be in an almost frozen, comatose state.

Mt. Baldy also had a major surprise at the unloading platform. This was not a standard chairlift where foot passengers would stand up and run like blazes down the ramp. This one-of-a-kind chair folded back and pivoted around the passengers. Unfortunately, the howling wind made it impossible for passengers to hear the unloading instructions being shouted by the lift operator. Unable to hear the unloading instructions, foot passengers would stand up and move to each side, thinking the chair would pass between them. Instead, the chair would hit them from behind and knock them flat on their faces.

In the late 1930s, Johnny Elvrum bought Snow Valley, its two ropetows and a "sling" lift for $850. For years he made more money renting toboggans than he did skis. Groups of people would load six or eight relatives on the toboggan and then hurtle toward imminent death or dismemberment against some very solid object at the bottom. Some of the best laughs in my early films were of these sopping-wet, T-shirt-

Skiers at Yosemite's Badger Pass paid 25 cents each to ride the Up-Ski, a boat-shaped sled that hauled them up the slope at the speed of a lethargic snail.

clad, pipe-smoking fathers with their already crying kids slamming into a tree, a rock or spectators.

The sling lift at Snow Valley was a different thrill. Imagine a steel cable about 15 feet in the air with four wires that held a horizontal 10-foot wooden two-by-four. Attached to the dangling two-by-fours were eight dangling slings made of discarded canvas fire hose. Eight skiers would line up and put the slings over their heads and down around their fannies. Once everyone had paid their 10 cents, a signal would be given to start the lift and all eight people were supposed to start up the hill at the same time.

As sure as there are tips on your skis, there would always be a first-time sling-rider on the lift. That person would inevitably fall halfway up and be dragged along until his or her screams could be heard by the mechanic who was running the ancient automobile engine that powered the lift. He would slip the engine out of gear, and then the seven standing skiers would start to slide back down the hill until the

WARRENISM

"My friend always speaks his mind, which, of course, limits his conversation."

mechanic jammed on the brake. If the brake worked, the lift would stop instantly and the seven standing skiers would fall over like dominos.

During and after World War II, skiers headed for Yosemite National Park, where they would take their chances on another unique ski lift.

Called the Up-Ski, it utilized a pair of boat-shaped sleds hauled by a steel cable. As one sled went up the mountain with skiers in it, the other came down empty. Twenty people at a time would pay 25 cents each to climb into the sled, stand their skis vertically in a ski rack in the center of the sled and be hauled up the hill at the speed of a lethargic snail.

One spring day the sled tipped over. Everyone fell or jumped out, and the sled continued up the hill with the skis. When it arrived at the top, it contained only the bottom halves of the skis. All 20 pairs of skis had been broken off at the bindings as the sled, still being dragged along on its side, had come too close to a tree.

What the Shah Didn't Know

In Deer Valley, Utah, a couple of weeks ago, I listened to the crackling of the hand-held radios being used by Secret Service men guarding President Bill Clinton, who was there on a $3.7 million learn-to-ski weekend with Chelsea and Hillary. It reminded me of a similar incident with a another head of state in Sun Valley, Idaho, many years ago.

The Shah of Iran had come to Sun Valley to ski with the ski school director, Sigi Engl. It was the winter of 1949-50, and I was already traveling and showing my first feature-length ski film to any group of two or more people that would sit still to watch it.

The Shah had brought 16 bodyguards with him from Iran, but none of them could ski, so the head of the ski patrol asked for volunteers who could handle a .45-caliber automatic pistol.

Four patrolmen seemed like the right number of men to handle the job. The designated four men were issued Army surplus automatic pistols and told to drive out to Warm Springs and practice firing a half dozen magazines and to be ready to ski the next morning.

Everything worked to perfection. Two of the patrolmen were skiing in front of the Shah and Sigi, while the other two skied behind them. After a few days of skiing like this, everyone at Sun Valley got used to the group, and the guards began to relax.

The Shah was a powerful skier, hurtling down almost any slope in a very wide snowplow. He had learned to ski on his own ski lift near Teheran and particularly enjoyed skiing in the moonlight. When Pat Rogers, Sun Valley's manager, heard about this, he arranged to have a party at the Roundhouse two-thirds of the way up the side of Baldy. After an evening of dancing, caviar, fine champagne and a full moon, the party got into their ski gear and, with torch blazing, skied down the canyon.

Those who couldn't handle night skiing got to ride down on the Exhibition lift; it was there that the first hint of trouble emerged. One of the men in the Shah's party hollered at his compatriot riding in front of him to throw him a half-full bottle of champagne to ward off the chill. Turning around in a single chair and throwing a bottle of champagne on a 50-foot upward slant is no mean task. The bottle flew through the air but was about two feet short of the catcher, who, as he reached out to grab it, fell out of the chair.

Halfway down Exhibition, this half-drunk Iranian who couldn't speak English was now stuck knee-deep in snow. By the time the ski patrol left the Roundhouse with the toboggan and got the drunk to the ambulance at the bottom of the hill, the sky was turning gray in the east. Had the Iranian not been so full of champagne, the evening could have turned out tragically.

The next day, during lunch in the Roundhouse, the ski patrolmen hung their automatic weapons on the clothes rack, covered them with their ski parkas, and went over to the cafeteria counter to order lunch. Watching this, a friend of mine said, "Why don't we switch parkas with them, take theirs and two of their guns, and see what'll happen."

I walked over with him and stood directly between the parkas, the guns and Sigi, the Shah and his guards. While I stood there, the instigator of this potential international incident switched our two, sort-of-the-same-color red parkas for theirs and draped them over two of the automatic pistols. He handed a parka and a gun to me, and we sauntered casually out the door, climbed into our skis and skied quickly down the Canyon and River Run.

At the bottom, we left the guns and holsters hanging on a fence, covered them with the ski patrol parkas, and told the lift operators to keep their eyes open for Sigi, the Shah and the four ski patrolmen later in the day.

The two patrolmen who couldn't find their guns wisely decided to just fake it for the rest of the day. Sigi and the Shah never did know that the firepower of their guards had been cut in half, and skied the rest of the afternoon in Christmas Bowl. When they got to the bottom of the River Run lift on their final run of the day, the lift operator hollered at the group as they skied by. One of the ski-patrol-guards-without-guns

WARRENISM

> **"Take your ski vacation the week after New Year's. That's when everyone is busy exchanging their Christmas presents for something they want."**

skied over and was very embarrassed when he was handed the two guns and parkas we had "borrowed" at lunch.

I couldn't help but wonder what today's ever present media would have had to say if a drunk had fallen off a chairlift or a prank with guns had been played during the Clintons' learn-to-ski vacation. Somehow I think that our journalists would have raised these incidents to the level of a national crisis, and Janet Reno would have ordered a multi-million dollar investigation.

Mysterious Ernest

Where Ernest came from I never really knew. He was on the ski patrol when I was living in the parking lot in Sun Valley, Idaho, during the winter of 1947. Ernest stood about five-feet, 10-inches tall, was very husky and good looking, with a thick head of straight, coal black hair and a dark complexion. And he was very, very quiet.

He moved with the calculated, simple grace of a mountain lion, and at parties he never drank or womanized—even though half of the female employees in Sun Valley were chasing after him. There were all kinds of rumors about his background, and when you were talking to him and looking into his dark brown, almost black, piercing eyes, you knew there was something very powerful lurking behind them, but there was no way you could read what it was. I don't think anyone in Sun Valley knew for sure what his real background was, but the oft-told story of his life went like this:

Ernest was rumored to have a full-blooded Sioux father and a mother who was French Canadian. He had served well in World War II as a scout in the famed Tenth Mountain Division ski troops. It was said that he carried no rifle with him to fight the war in Europe. He was uncanny with a bow and arrow: It was whispered that his skills had been passed down from his father, who learned them from his grandfather, Chief Flying Hawk, nephew of Sitting Bull and brother of Kicking Bear.

It was said, "With his bow and arrow, Ernest could shoot and kill small game from the back of a galloping horse—or while gliding through the trees in unpacked powder snow on his cross-country skis on a moonlit night."

Some even said, "Ernest could hit a bird in flight with his unwavering arrows."

Everyone in Sun Valley believed the stories, and they were probably even embellished as word spread, because you later heard that "Ernest had stolen behind enemy lines and killed more than a dozen enemy soldiers with his silent bow and deadly arrows."

Sometimes, in the Sun Valley employee cafeteria, when Ernest was sitting off in a corner by himself nursing a cup of black coffee, it was easy to imagine him at war, silently stealing through the trees and across the new fallen snow. At exactly the right moment in the black of night, with the almost noiseless twang of his bowstring, an unsuspecting sentry would topple over dead, one of Ernest's silent arrows sticking out of his chest just below the left collarbone—right through the heart. Then, just as silently, he would continue to map the perimeter defenses of the enemy lines, sneaking back across the lines before dawn and reporting to his sergeant, "It's all clear in the eastern sector for the next assault."

The first time I saw Ernest in action was going straight down The Ridge at about 45 mph while skiing upright between the handles of a 100-pound patrol toboggan with a seriously injured skier in it. When the patrol lined up in the early dawn to ski pack the Canyon, Ernest usually took twice as many sidesteps as the other patrollers and his line packed out a little better. Ernest always did a little more than he was asked—or paid—to do.

Only once did I ever witness Ernest's bow-and-arrow skills.

The ducks and geese that wintered at the head of Dollar Lake, near the bridge that ran over Trail Creek, were almost too fat to fly. They spent the winter living on large handouts of leftover food from the Sun Valley Lodge dining room. On occasion, however, a stray dog or guest would scare them up into flight and they would laboriously circle the Challenger Inn, all the while honking loudly enough to wake up Ward Baker and myself in our small trailer in the parking lot.

More than once during the Christmas and New Year's holidays, Ward and I were awakened by the loud honking of the obese geese. It always took them about three or four laps around the village to gain much altitude. Then, as if it was too much work to fly any longer, they would splash back down in the same small, unfrozen water where Trail Creek flowed into Dollar Lake to wait for their next handout.

In the gray dawn of the below-zero morning of December 31, we were awakened by all six of the Trail Creek geese in flight. One of them, however, sounded very different. His honking was high pitched and labored, almost wheezing. I didn't think too much about it, except that

I had never heard them fly this low over the parking lot before. I did know, however, that no one would go down to Trail Creek that early in the morning just to scare the geese and ducks so they could watch them fly over the village.

The second time the flock flew honking over our campground, I stuck my head out of the trailer door in time to catch another glimpse. Something was very wrong with one of them. Another goose was flying unusually close and his neck was at a very weird angle for the normal, graceful flight of a goose. Hoping they would circle once again, I climbed out of bed for a better look.

I didn't actually get out of my mummy sleeping bag; I just stood up in it in the snowbank outside the trailer and watched for them as they flew on their next round trip over the village. The goose with the peculiar sound and the strange bend in his neck had an arrow sticking through him. His breast was covered with blood, and it was obvious that he was going to crash somewhere soon.

It was later said that "Ernest had already poached a deer and an elk with his bow and arrow and had decided that a goose might add some variety to the menu of the annual Ski Patrol New Year's Eve big-game dinner."

In the Ski Patrol barracks, at about the same time the wounded goose crash-landed in front of the Opera House, Ernest was silently packing his clothes, his skis, his bow and his quiver with one arrow missing. He wasn't at the New Year's Eve party that night but was last seen walking south out of Ketchum with a very substantial load on his shoulders.

The Antelope Who Loved Cigarette Butts

O n the way to the village this morning, I drove along behind a 1950 Chevrolet panel truck exactly like the one I lived in for three years in the early 1950s—except that mine was fire-engine red. Seeing that truck brought back a lot of memories.

It was March 1951. I was in Sun Valley, Idaho, shooting the Harriman Cup races on Baldy. I'd even talked Hannes Schneider, the most famous skier of the pre-World War II era, into making a few turns for my then one-year-old film company.

At the moment my story begins, I was cooking dinner in my panel truck. The pressure cooker was hissing on my Coleman stove in the back of the truck when I heard a lot of screaming and shouting outside. Annie, the pet antelope that ate every cigarette butt she could find, was running our way. As she rounded a corner to get away from whoever had scared her, she slipped on some ice, slammed against the bumper of my truck and slid to a stop underneath it.

Not having much experience in getting a wounded antelope out from under a parked truck, I recruited the two kids who had been chasing her to help. With them sitting on the ice on the other side of my truck, I sat down, hung onto the running board and shoved Annie the Antelope out with my foot. By now a half-dozen people had gathered around with advice on how to handle this emergency. As soon as the two kids on the other side of the truck got a good hold of Annie, I scrambled to my feet and ran around to the other side. Before I got there I slipped on the same patch of ice, did a partial back flip and knocked the wind out of myself. Meanwhile, my helpers had demonstrated the proper way to keep a bleeding antelope on the ground while spraying antelope blood all over your clothes. Annie had a nasty cut on her

WARREN MILLER 02

shoulder where she'd hit my bumper, and she was covered with grease from the underside of my truck.

Since my helpers were already fairly bloody, the older kid held his hand over the wound while I took one of my ski-boot longthongs and tied the antelope's legs together. Next I wrestled Annie into my arms and headed for the hospital on the third floor of the Lodge, where I hoped to get one of the doctors to sew her up. Dr. Moritz was in surgery when I arrived and the nurse on duty refused to do the emergency repair job herself. But she was nice enough to draw a diagram of how and where to start sewing up the wound and to tie the right kind of knot—and she sneaked sutures and a needle into my bloody parka pocket. We took the passenger elevator down to the lobby, then left a trail of blood from there to my truck. We laid the wounded antelope down in front of my headlights and sewed up Annie's shoulder. By now the thermometer had dropped to about four degrees above zero, and my fingers were very stiff as I tried several times to duplicate the knot the nurse had shown me. Finally I untied Annie's legs. She lay there gasping for a few moments, then struggled to her feet and slowly staggered off into the darkness.

The following winter Annie was found dead near Dollar Lake. She showed no gunshot wounds or other apparent cause of death. A ski patrolman who worked part time as a veterinarian's assistant performed an autopsy and declared that Annie had died of cancer of the stomach—from eating too many cigarette butts.

Those Crafty French

On a rainy, snowy day in March 1955, I drove 16 long hours in a borrowed Volkswagen bug from Innsbruck, Austria, over the Arlberg Pass, through Liechtenstein and Zurich, Switzerland, on to Geneva and into France. I was in search of a new ski resort that wasn't yet on the Michelin roadmaps.

It was called Courchevel 1850. The designer of this new resort was my old friend and three-time world skiing champion Emile Allais. I had worked with Emile at Sun Valley, Idaho, during the winter of 1948-49, where he had taught the top racing class and I had taught the people who had never skied a day in their lives. The next winter I joined Emile at the then new ski resort, Squaw Valley, California.

Just after midnight when I finally arrived at Courchevel 1850, I stopped in front of the only light burning in town. My knowledge of the French language at that time was limited to pointing at my mouth when I wanted food and pretending to fall asleep when I wanted a room. Somehow, in that smoke-filled bar, the very drunk bartender understood what I wanted and directed me to a dingy upstairs room right over the jukebox.

The next morning I somehow located Emile, and for the next four or five days, with my rucksack, my skis and my camera, Emile and I and a young ski patrolman named Jean Catilan skied and filmed unbelievable powder snow. I learned a lot about ski resort planning in those four or five days as Emile and I filmed, reminisced and talked about what ski resorts would be like 30 or 40 years in the furure.

The French had—and still have—a very different attitude than Americans do about winter tourism as an industry. During World War II, some former ski racers who flew for the French Air Force observed a

lot of high mountain meadows that had no roads leading up to them. After the war they convinced the government that there was a big future for winter tourism. All the government had to do was buy those high meadows from the farmers and then build roads up to these ski resorts of the future.

The French government did just that.

To spur hotel growth, the government would give a good site to a developer if he would build a certain number of hotel rooms within one year. The concept was simple: If the developer didn't have to spend millions of francs for the land, he could build a lot more hotel rooms. The

"A million dollars doesn't always bring happiness. A man with a $10 million house in Aspen is no happier than a man with a $9 million house in Sun Valley."

ski resorts grew rapidly, and I was privileged to ski there and document the growth with my camera.

The first year I visited Courchevel it had a gondola, three or four surface lifts and slept less than 800 people. When I returned a year later to spend more time with Emile, Courchevel had a couple of thousand more hotel rooms and eight or 10 more lifts.

Some of the lifts resembled dangling Roman chariots without wheels. Each chariot hung from a moving cable, just like a chair on a chairlift, but to get on this lift you had to take your skis off and run like crazy as the chariot came by, then jump aboard and stand there to be hauled skyward. The "dangling chariots," as I called them that year in my movie, now connected the village of Courchevel 1850 with the village in the next valley, Meribel. You could ski back and forth between the villages. You could stay in one village and ski in the other. You could eat breakfast and dinner in one resort and have lunch in the other.

This was a new concept in ski resort development.

Each year that I went back to film Emile, there were more and more lifts added to the resort complex. Sometime during the 1960s they even built an airport halfway up the side of the one of the ski runs. Now you could fly up from Geneva or Paris in a Pilotus Porter (a short take-off and landing aircraft) and be met by a porter who would carry your luggage to your hotel, give you a lift ticket, provide a report on the snow conditions and arrange for a licensed guide to show you around if you wanted one.

Within 12 years of my first visit, the resort had grown to include a third village, Les Menuire. The complex is now known as Les Trois Valles.

The Three Valleys.

You can ski 14 airline miles from one town to the other and take your choice of 214 lifts. In the complex there are almost a quarter of a million pillows. That's about 1,200 skiers for each lift, provided they are all skiing at once.

But of course they never are.

Half the guests are sitting in the sun on a porch after a three-hour lunch. Twenty percent are shopping. Ten percent are drinking. Another 10 percent are asleep, getting ready to dance and drink all night. The remaining 10 percent are riding one of the 214 lifts, and some of them are skiing from village to village.

This village-to-village concept is so popular in Europe, it's hard to understand why American resorts haven't followed their lead.

For example: Why not connect Squaw Valley and Alpine Meadows? Park City, Deer Valley and The Canyons? Or Park City and Brighton and Solitude? Or Vail and Beaver Creek?

Why not? The French have been doing it for almost 50 years.

Impasse in a Crevasse

The tram was crowded as it climbed rapidly in the clear blue French sky. The 22 inches of new powder snow had gotten everyone in town up early. Waiting in line took longer than normal because of the early birds with inside connections. Private instructors with their pupils and the spousal equivalents of ski patrolmen were already crowding in line ahead of me for their second run in the untracked powder.

The Super Chamonix upper tram has a cable speed of almost 20 miles per hour, so once on board the 5,000-vertical-foot ride takes less than 10 minutes. As it swayed gently and glided over the main tower, we could see a group of four skiers traversing over the top of one of the best slopes on this vast, undulating steep glacier. Not another ski track was yet visible on the west side of the gondola except their traverse marks.

Under the foot and a half of light powder that fell is a glacier of rock-hard ice that is over 500 feet deep in places. It is criss-crossed by deep crevasses. The mile-long sea of ice doesn't bend but instead breaks as the mountain's shape changes the course of the ice as it moves. The crevasses are sometimes as wide as a 100 feet or so, or as narrow as an inch or two and sometimes seemingly limitless in their depth. When it snows hard, the blowing snow forms a cornice on one side of the crevasse and, when the wind changes direction, it forms another cornice on the other side of the crevasse. The two cornices grow larger and larger until they sometimes touch and form a bridge of snow. There is nothing underneath the bridge except a seemingly bottomless void. Where the two cornices meet is sometimes only an inch or two thick, so when a skier goes across one, the fragile bridge of snow can give way and the skier can fall to their death.

I was explaining all of this to a friend as I watched the four skiers traversing the glacier. One of the ladies in the group, who was wearing a canary-yellow parka, was traversing a little higher than the other three when she suddenly disappeared, her long traverse tracks ending in a black hole the size of a pair of skis and her body.

Fortunately, the conductor on the tram witnessed the accident and quickly dialed the ski patrol. By the time we arrived at the top station, the ski patrol was on its way down to attempt a rescue.

For me this was a good opportunity to get some rare rescue shots for a magazine article I was writing. I skied down as fast as I could in the deep snow; by the time I got to the accident, half of the patrol was engaged in crowd control. At least half a dozen other ski patrolmen had rigged rescue ropes and lowered one of the patrolmen down into the crevasse. The word he sent up from deep in the crevasse was encouraging. A lady had fallen in. She was down about 45 feet, perched precariously on a narrow ledge of ice that fortunately was covered with about five feet of powder snow. She was stunned but still alive. For the next 10 minutes there was much hollering back and forth from the patrolman who was in charge to the one down in the crevasse who was actually doing all of the rescue work.

A few minutes later, the head patrolman said something untranslatable in French, and the five remaining patrolmen began sidestepping down the hill. They all had a good grip on the rope that led down to the lady in the crevasse.

When the victim finally was dragged over the lip of the crevasse, we were all shocked to discover that it wasn't the lady in the yellow parka that we had expected to see.

Instead, on the end of the rope was a man. It turned out he had fallen into the crevasse two days earlier and was near death from hypothermia. Fortunately, he had been wearing a thick down parka over his powder suit and long underwear. He also had two candy bars with him, and the combination had saved his life. However, he had wasted away to virtual skin and bone. He looked like he had lost 20 pounds during his two-day ordeal in the darkness of the sub-zero crevasse. When this hypothermia-caused-weight-loss information was passed back down to the ski patrolman who was still in the crevasse, a heated argument was heard between the patrolman and the lady who was still down there.

Armed with the information that the guy they had hauled up first had lost 20 pounds while down in the crevasse, she hollered back up, "Come back and get me in a couple of days!"

SHORT SWINGS

Freedom

In 1919, soon after World War I, Hannes Schneider of St. Anton, Austria, said, "If everyone skied, there would be no wars." Two decades later, Schneider escaped religious persecution from a non-skiing madman and fled to the U.S. He spread his knowledge of ski technique and freedom at Mt. Cranmore, New Hampshire, thus becoming the father of American ski instruction.

I first read Hannes' words while I was living in a parking lot in Sun Valley, Idaho, in 1947. They were true when he spoke them in 1919, they were true at the outbreak of World War II they were true in 1947, and they are still true today.

Man's fundamental drive is his search for freedom. For no reason that I can explain, some people—especially skiers—answer to that instinctive search for freedom more than others. My skis have taken me to the many corners of the world in my own search for freedom. During my first winter of skiing in Sun Valley, I learned that I could dine on free oyster crackers and ketchup for lunch, then ride on the same chairlift with Gary Cooper and his wife—or even Averell Harriman, the president of Union Pacific Railroad and founder of the resort. When we got to the top, we were all equals. When we weren't skiing, Gary and his wife were paying the then unheard-of price of $30 a night for a room in the lodge with a fireplace. My fireplace was the Coleman stove out behind my eight-foot-long trailer that I cooked dinner on. We were still equals, though I was a little colder.

Last winter, the Warren Miller film company sent a camera crew and skiers to Iran. They discovered a ski resort there that had some lifts for men only and some lifts for women only. But the lifts went to the top of the same hill, so that men and women, though segregated by law,

found equality on the slopes.

Even though Iranian religion and culture are radically different from ours, the Warren Miller crew bonded with the locals. Was that because the cameramen got to ride on the women's lift—and the sky still didn't fall down? Or because they shared a passion for skiing, and the freedom and equality that goes with the sport? The camera crew got great footage of both the men and the women skiing, even though the women of Iran were treated as second-class citizens—regardless of the financial status of their husbands or fathers.

The same thing that occurred in Iran happened to me in Sun Valley, when my pair of skis broke down the barriers between myself and Gary Cooper...and even the man who created Sun Valley. At the top of any ski hill, gravity makes a mockery of what the various governments stand for—and further emphasizes what Hannes Schneider said more than 80 years ago.

I can remember my first day on a pair of skis, and so can you—no matter how long ago it was. For me it was in 1937, at the end of a dirt road that led to Mt. Waterman, California. Two years later, a chairlift was installed that would later provide freedom for a lot of soldiers and sailors on leave during World War II, myself included.

In 1945, I had earned some leave from the Navy because our ship was sunk in a hurricane in the South Pacific just before the war ended. I spent every day of my leave on a ropetow in Yosemite. I knew I was going to be sent back overseas again, but during that leave. I was free to ski as much and as fast as my adrenaline would allow.

What is closer to total freedom and equality than two skiers standing on a summit with blue sky overhead and a long steep mountain of untracked powder snow below? You can go wherever you want, at whatever speed you want, using any style you want. And whoever you are skiing with will be waiting for you when you get there. It doesn't really matter who gets there first, because both of you have your freedom on the way down.

When Hannes Schneider said, "If everyone skied, there would be no wars" in 1919, there were no ski lifts of any kind, not even ropetows. The only way to get up a hill was by putting one foot in front of the other. There were no metal edges, metal skis, safety bindings, plastic boots, condominiums, snowmaking machines, rental cars, video ski lessons, aluminum ski poles, waterproof clothes or crash helmets. But the essence of skiing was still the same then, and each of the above was invented to help us enjoy it even more.

I wonder what would have happened if Osama bin Laden had bought a pair of skis and built a chairlift with all his money—instead of an AK-47 and a passport to Afghanistan.

Christmas

I f I were any luckier, I would have to be two people, because I've been able to spend the past 52 Christmases skiing somewhere in the world. I used to spend some of that time running my movie camera, so I could share the sunshine and snow with people who might not have had either. During my Christmas vacations, I've skied and filmed powder snow, blue ice, corn snow, very little snow and no snow. And I've learned quite a few lessons along the way, both on and off the slopes.

Christmas Day, 1958, I watched three instructors trying to thread their classes down the Half Dollar ski hill with the rest of Sun Valley shut down because of tall sage brush and very little snow. Talking to Sepp, the ski school manager, I said, "You ought to look into those new snowmaking machines I just filmed, like the one Walt Stopa has at Wilmot in Wisconsin." Sepp's answer was, "Those snowmaking machines are okay for those back-east ski resorts. But we don't need them here in Idaho, where we get a lot of snow."

Today, almost every ski resort in America has snowmaking machinery and some even start them up in September so they can offer skiing by Halloween. A lot of skiers are upset if they don't have great skiing by Thanksgiving, much less Christmas. And if it hasn't dumped seven feet of snow by New Year's Eve, those same skiers write off the winter as a bad one. Personally, I try to spend the early season looking for the snow between the rocks.

As my three children grew in age and size, we kept up the Christmas road-trip tradition. It was always hard to finish up a 75-city tour with my feature ski film, have three days to get caught up in the office, pack the car with our skis and luggage and start driving 900

miles to spend Christmas in the mountains. But after driving for 18 hours on four hours sleep, the magic of looking out the ski lodge window in the predawn darkness and seeing new powder snow always erased any fatigue and frustration I might have brought with me. Later, while walking to breakfast with my children, feeling the crunch of snow under our feet, seeing our breath in the clean mountain air, throwing snowballs at each other and listening to the distant boom of avalanche guns, my life always got back into focus. No one can ever take those holiday memories away from me or my family.

But in recent years, something different has been happening around the base of the ski hill on Christmas day. I hear it in childrens' voices. It's a different attitude.

"My Christmas tree has more presents under it than yours."

"Tommy has a more expensive ____ (fill in the blank) than I do."

Materialism is creeping into people at much too young an age. Does it come from the parents' attitude that their condo is bigger than yours? There used to be a saying about "Keeping up with the Joneses." Why not just be one of the Joneses? Then if anyone wants to try to keep up with you, let it be when you're carving first tracks on a powder morning.

I have seen wives send their husbands' corporate jet back to their hometown to pick up a special dress they forgot to include in the 19 suitcases of clothes they brought for the many Christmas parties. A friend once told me that her husband had given her a parachute for Christmas. I was a little surprised because she was not the skydiving type. She explained that her husband had given her a parachute—not for personal use but for their jet, so they could land at airports with shorter runways and wouldn't have to spend so much time in the limo getting to the ski resort.

Everyone has at least one story for every Christmas of his or her life. One year, just after the holidays, I was filming a celebrity ski race and met a young lady named Tracy Taylor. She was the March of Dimes poster girl that year. She was born with spina bifida, which causes paralysis, and at the age of 11 she was no bigger than a minute.

After the opening ceremonies, she had her picture taken in the arms of each celebrity, and when the photoshoot was over, I held her in my arms and skied over to where her mom was sitting. Tracy was wearing plaster casts from her toes to her hips, and when I put her down in her wheel chair, I turned to her mother and asked, "How much does Tracy weigh?"

"About 35 pounds."

"That's about the same as one of my movie cameras with a tripod. Would you let Tracy take a ski run with me?"

Without hesitation her mom answered, "Sure."

I picked Tracy up in my arms and coasted over to the chairlift.

Taking advantage of the ski school line, we jumped right onto the chair and started for the top of the mountain. When I began skiing down with her cradled in my arms, her pencil-thin arms were wrapped tightly around my neck. Before I had made a half dozen turns, her death-grip around my neck began to ease, and within 100 yards she was waving at anyone who was standing alongside the ski run.

Tracy had a spirit that I have never seen in another human. By the time we got to the bottom of the hill, word had spread, and people were cheering her every time we made a turn. Tracy was hooting and hollering and giving everyone the thumbs up.

On the next run, as we gently cruised over the smaller bumps, I alternately held her down between my legs or lifted her high above my head, pretending she was getting big air. At the age of 11, Tracy had become an extreme skier.

Two weeks later, I made arrangements for Tracy to fly to Denver and go to ski school with Hal O'Leary in Winter Park, Colorado. Hal pretty much invented handicapped ski instruction, and he taught her how to ski down a hill all by herself. During her whole life, she had never been able to walk without crutches and braces, yet after her first nonstop ski run on the fourth day she said, "God made me this way on purpose so I can prove to the world that anyone can do anything they want to do."

What are you going to be doing this Christmas season? How about spending a day giving some ski lessons to people who might not be able to afford a day on the hill? All it takes is some of your time and some of your old equipment that's rusting in your garage. How about talking your favorite ski resort manager into letting everyone ride the resort's short, flat, beginner chairlift all day for a $10 bill and throwing in the free use of some of last year's rental ski equipment at the same time?

I remember one very special Christmas Eve almost 50 years ago. My young wife had just died of cancer and our son was barely a year-and-a-half old. I was heading back to my hotel room alone in a blizzard

"There is something about a camera that lowers a skier's I.Q."

with the wind blowing 25 mph and the single stoplight in town swing-ing in the wind. As I waited for the signal to change, I glanced over at the curb. At 2:30 on Christmas morning there was an elderly man sit-ting on a bench in the blowing snow waiting for the bus with his seeing eye dog.

I drove about half a mile before I was able to make a U-turn and go back to offer the blind man and his dog a ride. I was across the street when a big red van pulled up and the man with the white and red cane and his dog climbed aboard. The van driver was a very fat man with long white hair, a big white beard and a twinkle in his eye.

He looked over at me as they drove away together, and I realized on that Christmas morning that if I were any luckier I would have to be two people.

Buzzwords

On a recent flight, I sat next to a young woman who was headed to Aspen for her first "Learn to Ski" week. After being served the standard miniature airline meal, she pulled out an issue of *SKI* Magazine from the seat pocket in front of her. She couldn't understand any of what she was reading, so I offered my years of experience to help her learn the Buzzwords of Skiing.

Heliskiing. An exotic, noisy and extremely expensive way to become the most listened to person on the summer cocktail circuit.

Buddy Pass. What ski resorts sell when they realize they can't charge what the "market will bear" because there no longer is a market.

All-Mountain Expert. Someone who lives in his van, can forge any lift ticket ever invented and hauls people from one ski resort to the next in exchange for gas and beer money.

Full-Spectrum Twin-Cam. A pair of twins who run a color video company at Big Sky, Montana, and will video you skiing for $100 an hour or two runs—whichever takes longer.

Quad Lift. A multi-million-dollar device that floats through the air at a high rate of speed and that you can cling to during a blizzard for what seems like hours. With luck, you won't be sitting downwind from three strangers who are smoking something other than tobacco and haven't had a bath since they left home two days ago.

Timeshare. A mathematical formula in which someone can buy two weeks of a year in a ski resort condo. The available weeks are either early November or right after the lifts close in April.

Manmade Snow. A technology that uses vast amounts of electricity to expensively convert water into ice on the side of a steep hill. This allows you to pay up to $67 dollars a day to wait in line and look at it

A Powder Hound's timeshare as he's racking up Skier Days on a Buddy Pass.

while a college graduate who is earning $9 an hour tries to convert the warm water coming out of the nozzles into powder snow.

Skier Days. The supposedly exact number of all-day lift tickets sold at a given resort during the winter. It's a number that is flexible enough so that the last person to be the marketing director in the spring can always exaggerate the number and hold his job through the summer.

Conquer the Elements. What you'll do with your rain slicker and umbrella when the temperature rises 40 degrees on your weeklong ski vacation at Mt. Bellyache and the forecasted two feet of powder turns out to be several inches of rain.

Insurance. A mysterious piece of paper that allows ambulance-chasing attorneys to write off their vacations while listening to the ski patrol radio channel to monitor accidents. This automatically increases the cost of your lift ticket by 25 percent.

Travel Agency. The company that books you into the wrong room at the wrong hotel at the wrong end of town at the wrong time of the year at the wrong price when the snow level is down to 9,000 feet and the next storm isn't coming until the morning of your departing flight.

Public Relations Director. Someone who sold used cars before he washed dishes before he joined the ski patrol and saved the injured wife of the owner of Mt. Bellyache.

Merger. When two ski resorts with three years of bad snow climb on the same toboggan to ride downhill on what's left of their financial statement.

Pisten Bully. A quarter of a million dollar device that smooths out all of the bumps in the snow. Anyone over the age of 40 would have quit skiing if it had not been invented.

Snow Gun. A very expensive device used to spray small drops of water onto rocks and stumps so they can, under a mild drop in temperature, slowly coagulate into homogenous frozen, icy masses the size of subcompact cars.

Snow Report. An ambiguous hypothesis of potential snow conditions by the assistant marketing director who has a masters degree in creative writing and is looking for a better paying job.

Cellular Phone. A cheaply produced electronic gizmo that someone invented so a ski vacation can now be tax deductible by having your assistant phone you every morning at 11:10 while you are riding the lift with three other people who are talking on their exotic phones to their assistants.

Artificial Insulating Fiber. Something that cost a company $14.7 million in R&D so it can duplicate the feathers of a Chinese duck that would have cost 45 cents.

ABS Brakes. These initials stand for "always brake slowly" or you will skid. And if you do brake slowly, you will hit the driver in front of you who jammed on his ABS brakes.

Powder Hounds. A semi-rare breed of hot dog that spends all winter trying to track up new powder snow.

"Single." A 53-year-old divorced man wearing a gold chain and sporting a hair transplant who is searching for a lift-riding companion, a free dinner and lodging for the night while he searches for his next ex-wife.

Cross-Training. A semi-religious rite performed while bathed in sweat for the upcoming season's sport. Real cross-trainers never compete in seasonal sports because they are always cross-training for the season to come.

Special Discount. The mystical and hypothetical discount that is subtracted from the supposed retail price of any ski product after the normal markup has been doubled.

Skid Chains. A device that is impossible to put on your car wheels, especially when the Highway Patrol tells you to. However, there is always a man standing at the chain-control sign in a yellow slicker who will put them on for you for a pair of $20 bills—if, that is, you remembered to put chains in the trunk. If not, you can buy a new set for $100.

Pill-Resistant, Chill-Resistant Fabric. Wear this parka and you will never have to take any more drugs and your sweat will drown you before the cold freezes you.

Power Vacuum Tech. How your room gets clean when you're skiing. That is if the maid shows up on time, which he or she probably won't because this is a powder snow day.

Mogul. A hugely successful tycoon who is in any business except skiing.

Don't Keep Score

Like our ancient ancestors, human beings are still hunter-gatherers. Today's men and women hunt and gather sports trophies and records. They try to run farther, jump higher, ski faster, ride or swim quicker than the next person, always pushing the limits, trying to be better than those around them.

However, most of us refuse to accept the fact that our bodies are aging before our eyes. There was a time in college when I could play nonstop basketball for three or four hours and not be tired. I could paddle a 100-pound redwood surfboard all day long and stay in the water for hours without a wetsuit. But eventually age caught up with me.

In 1962, after surfing for 25 years, I gave it up and started racing sailboats. The race courses were not nearly as crowded as the waves in Southern California, and the wind blew almost every day. Plus, racing that catamaran didn't require the agility of a teenager. I raced sailboats for the next 20 years, until I started getting beaten regularly by men and women 20 years younger than myself. Then I moved on.

To windsurfing.

Here was a challenge for anyone, regardless of age, or so I thought. I even moved to Maui for three months out of the year so I could do as much windsurfing as possible before my body wore out. But I was already in my 60s and soon came to realize I would never ride the giant waves at Hookipa—all I could do was surf the small ones in front of my condo. Slowly it came into focus that my pursuit of any particular sport was changing at the same rate that my body was wearing out. I finally gave up windsurfing, because it was just too hard on my body.

A few years ago I pedaled my mountain bike to the top of Vail Mountain and then coasted down. I didn't enjoy pedaling up, but I real-

ly enjoyed coasting down. That was about the same time Vail announced they would haul you and your mountain bike to the top for a $5 bill. My wife and I spent $10 one day and did just that. We coasted from the top of Lionshead to Mid Vail, where we had a nice lunch, and then coasted on down the construction roads to the village. In route we passed a lot of sweating people pedaling up. We also passed the bike patrol administering first aid to a tourist who had hit a tree on the way down. We coasted all the way back to our Vail home without turning a pedal. We didn't set any speed records, but I loved how the wind felt on my face as I coasted down, and the money I saved on my top-of-the-line Wal-Mart mountain bike allowed me to spend more on better ski equipment later on.

When it comes to skiing, I have long maintained that bumps on the hill are like heartbeats. You only have so many of them in your knees, and when they're gone, they're gone. My knees wore out a long time ago, and since bumps make you turn in specific places and take away all the freedom that skiing has to offer, I avoid bumps the way I avoid political discussions. Yes, I would still like to be able to jump cliffs and ski chest-deep powder, but my body won't do that anymore. Come to think of it, my body never did jump cliffs—I just filmed other people doing that. But because of snow grooming, I can still ski down a hill at a speed that gets my adrenaline going.

Is there a moral to this story? No.

There is a lesson, though: Don't try to be the oldest person in your sport. Move on to something that is a little easier on your body and gives a boost to your confidence. No one's keeping score except you. Are you the fastest person in the over-50 age group to run up Baldy in your underwear? Does anyone really care?

As I get older, I measure my athletic achievements by how wide my smile is. This won't give you bragging rights when you're sitting around the campfire at the senior citizens' trailer park in Arizona, but it does keep life interesting.

Don't give up on athletics altogether, just move on to a kinder, gentler sport. Keep adding new adult toys to your garage, while you give the older toys to a younger person. And the moment you get upset because you're not leading the pack, start over with some kinder, gentler sport.

A few years ago a young Norwegian rode his mountain bike from Norway to Nepal, towing all his climbing equipment in a small trailer. Then he climbed Mt. Everest alone, took pictures at the summit, climbed back down, and pedaled his bike back to Norway. There's a lesson in this story: No matter what your sport, there will always be somebody who can do it better.

Never mind keeping score.

Get In Shape

Hundreds of books, videotapes and magazine articles have been written and filmed about how to get your flabby body in perfect shape so it can be covered up with baggy ski clothes. A lot of those people with perfect bodies have made millions of dollars with their exercise tapes, books and health food, though I'm not sure anyone is actually thinner as a result.

I have skied for most of my life, and I recall doing a push-up once a few years ago, but I got carpet lint on my T-shirt, so I gave it up. I even bought some vitamins once, and their curative powers are still stored in a bottle somewhere in the garage with some other souvenirs of my occasional health binges.

Here are a few of my favorite ways to get in shape to ski and, just as important, to get in shape to get to where the skiing is.

Preparing for Takeoff: To get ready for your next international ski vacation flight, find a cardboard box for a 24-inch television set and put it in the middle of the living room. Climb into the box each night after a hard day at the office. Have a couple of things to drink and read alongside the box. Make sure that the coffee is cold and the cold drinks are warm.

After your legs go to sleep curled up in the box, have your spousal equivalent serve you a five-day-old, barely warm TV dinner. Make sure you use plastic knives and forks from last summer's picnic. After you spill the cold coffee all over your shirt, and with the empty dishes still in your lap, try to stay awake during three and a half hours of network TV rejects. (No remote channel changers allowed.) Make sure you watch it without sound, because earphones cost $4 extra.

When your body is asleep almost up to your armpits, the bath-

room is occupied and you can handle five and a half hours in the cardboard box, you are now ready to buy that 11-months-in-advance-discount ticket to Mt. Trashmore. (As if this isn't irritating enough, we now learn that long flights can cause serious circulatory problems. The solution: Inform the airline that you have a minor prostate problem, request an aisle seat and take frequent trips to the bathroom.)

Getting Down for Après-Ski Disco: In your bathroom at home, do 3,000 deep knee bends in one hour in a quilted parka. Do this with the heat turned up. When you are able to do 3,000 without sweating, you are ready for disco dancing. Do it to the beat of fast music, and eventually you will find that the only thing all of this gyrating, jumping and grooving does is shake the wrinkles out of your long underwear.

Getting In Shape for the 500-Mile Family Drive to Mt. Stupid: Buy two Sony Walkmans and put an ear piece from each one in either ear. Turn up the volume on two different rap CDs while also listening to your wife give directions to a Sunday afternoon party at your mother-in-law's house as your kids argue in the back seat.

Ready, Set, Helmet: Buy a five-pound bag of sugar or flour and put it into an empty 10-pound bag. Each morning when you go jogging, wear the bag on the top of your head. When you feel safe crossing the street without looking, you are in shape to ski with a helmet.

Luggage Lugging: Fill up your four largest suitcases with plastic bottles of expensive designer water. Put one suitcase under each arm and one in each hand with your skis in a bag over one shoulder and your boot bag over the other shoulder. Then jog as far as possible to the point of exhaustion, rest for 45 seconds and then repeat.

Liftline Standing: To prepare for waiting in liftlines, get a weekend job at Costco rearranging the frozen turkeys in the freezers. Do it without wearing gloves, and douse your face with cold water every time you enter the freezer.

The Condo Sofa-Bed Crunch: Roll up two large beach towels and put them in between your mattress and box spring right where your waist will be when you try to fall sleep. Fill your pillow with seven pounds of sand and then place a two-foot-wide box at the end of your bed so you can't stretch out.

Lunch-Tray Juggling: During half-time at a football game, fill up a tray with six plastic glasses of soda, three bowls of clam chowder, four hamburgers, six orders of fries and two orders of nachos. Then try to get back to your seat without spilling anything on anyone you are climbing over. Don't forget to wear your ski boots.

First-Tracks Imaging: When the weatherman says "rain tomorrow," set your alarm for 4:30 a.m. and get dressed in all of your ski clothes. Eat a quick breakfast of cold eggs and greasy bacon that you cooked the night before and then go outside and stand in the rain in the

WARRENISM

"One man's powder is another man's ice."

dark and convince yourself that it is snowing up at the top of your imaginary chairlift and that you are the first person in the liftline.

Heli-Ski Financial Planning: Pay off all of your credit cards and then burn them. For the next two to three years eat nothing for breakfast but oatmeal, nothing for lunch except peanut butter sandwiches and nothing at night except Kraft dinners. Drink nothing but water the entire time. During that same time get in good enough shape so that you can do 31,420 deep knee bends every day, for six days in a row, while sleeping only five hours a night.

Parking Lot Payola: Buy a pair of crutches and three ace bandages. Wrap up your wife's or husband's leg before you leave the motel, your home or the nearby condo. Make sure that the crutches can be seen propped up in the front seat of the car. When you enter the parking lot, give the $7-an-hour attendant a $10 bill so your companion with the crutches won't have to walk so far on the ice and snow.

Once you've finished this exclusive, trademarked Warren Miller workout, relax. You won't have to do it for another year.

The Presidential
Ski Weekend

The flashing lights of the Utah state police appeared in my rearview mirror one spring day in 1997. The police car's loudspeaker blared, "Turn off at the next off ramp." I did as I was told and was surprised when the police car didn't follow me off the freeway. Two minutes later, what seemed like a dozen or more black vehicles, all bearing U.S. government license plates, sped by. President Bill Clinton, together with your tax dollars, was bringing Chelsea and Hillary to Deer Valley, Utah, for a Learn to Ski Weekend.

According to most of the Republican bean counters in the state of Utah, who monitored every tax dollar spent, it turned out to be the most expensive Learn to Ski Weekend in history.

Let's start with transportation. On Thursday, the President and Hillary flew from Washington, D.C., to Stanford University in Palo Alto, California, to pick up Chelsea. Then they turned around and flew to Salt Lake City, Utah. On Sunday night, Air Force One jetted Chelsea back to Stanford and then returned to Washington, D.C., to drop off Bill and Hillary at the White House.

Air Force One has a fixed daily operating overhead of $37,000.00, not including mileage. There is also an Air Force Two that flies everywhere Air Force One goes. This is in case Air Force One runs off of the runway or the bedrooms are all occupied. That's another $37,000.00 a day for the second plane, which doesn't include the cost per mile to fly each of the 747s, nor does it include the dozens of army soldiers who guard the two planes 24 hours a day when they are parked.

Add to these costs the many technicians on board who keep in touch with goings on around the world, as well as three shifts of half a dozen Secret Service agents with earplugs and concealed weapons to guard the First Family. Also not included in the bill was the cost of a dozen or more Learn to Ski Weeks to teach the Secret Service agents how to ski in front of, and behind, Chelsea and Hillary as they lurched down the beginner's slopes at speeds that sometimes approached six miles per hour. These Secret Service agents' Learn to Ski Weeks had to occur at the resort where Hillary and Chelsea would be skiing so they could pick out the runs that would be safe from any onlookers or hidden cameramen. The instruction cost about $1,200 per security guard and didn't include their flight out on special government jet aircraft. Twelve times $1,200 is another $14,400 to add to the President's Learn to Ski Weekend bill.

There were a reported 136 people in the White House family entourage who descended on Deer Valley. This group included guards, cooks, advisors and attorneys, as well as some technicians, whose only job was to make sure the First Family's edges were sharp and their bindings adjusted exactly right. All of them had to be flown out from Washington, D.C., and housed and fed in previously secured condos.

They also had to be driven from the Salt Lake City airport to Deer Valley, so your tax dollars also had to fly eight bulletproof limousines from Washington, D.C., on a C-147 cargo plane. This massive airplane costs about as much to operate per day as Air Force One, so tack on an additional $37,000.00 per day, plus mileage.

The Ski Weekend consisted of Hillary and Chelsea doing a little traversing and kick-turning on a ski slope where no one else was allowed, except two instructors and six Secret Service men, while Bill relaxed in a Democratic party donor's very large house and caught up on his reading and cigar smoking. The press reported that Bill read his latest fan mail and tried to calculate the number of jokes that had been written about him since he took office. Remember that this was during the Monica Lewinsky days when he was trying to understand the meaning of "is."

On Sunday morning, anyone who had not previously been cleared by the CIA and the FBI was asked to leave downtown Park City

because Bill wanted to go downtown and mingle with the skiers. No snowboarders, please. This forced the closing of about half of the retail shops in town, because there were so many ski bums without green cards from half a dozen different countries working in them (these people are sometimes called "illegal aliens").

While Hillary and Chelsea tried to traverse and kick-turn on the absolute beginner's hill, President Bill Clinton was chauffeured to downtown Park City from Deer Valley in one of the many bulletproof limousines that had been flown out from Washington, D.C., for just such spur-of-the-moment, mingle-with-the-masses side trips. Once there, he commented on how few people were in town. Of course, his advisors forgot to tell him that everyone would be up riding the chair-lifts at 11:30 on a sunny powder snow morning.

In town, Bill had a cup of coffee, no cream, while the TV cameras took sound bites of his "pressing the flesh of Democratic Utah voters." It was also reported that the president tried to buy a book with his credit card, but the card had expired shortly after he took office. So an aide paid for the book.

While all of this was going on, there was a small group of Utah Republicans who were keeping track of how much the weekend was costing American taxpayers. When they added up the expenses of the White House staff, Air Force One, Air Force Two and the C-147 for four days and the round-the-clock army guards to protect them from souvenir hunters, the final tally for the First Family Learn to Ski Weekend was reported to be $5.7 million—almost enough to purchase the six-bedroom house they were staying in.

This is about $1 million more than was raised to build the original streets, the water and sewer systems, the powerlines and the first gondola and chairlifts so that Vail could open in 1962. It's also enough money to teach about 114,000 novices to ski, if you consider that discounted two-day Learn to Ski packages cost as little as $50 today.

Suddenly, I think I need a vacation.

Insecurities List

My research team tells me that no matter how many years people have been skiing, most are still insecure about the sport. Here are some of the reasons that we uncovered in our recent tax-deductible information-gathering trip to seven destination ski resorts.

1) You are midway between the two tallest lift towers when the chair-lift stops and all the chairs slide back 50 feet before the lift operator slams on the brakes. You bounce up and down the same way you did when you went bungee jumping.

2) You meet your private instructor who charges $420 a day for lessons and discover that she is two years younger than your youngest daughter.

3) You order lunch for two in the mountaintop restaurant with your new lady friend when you discover that you only have $30 in your pocket and no credit card.

4) You discover at 4:35 a.m. on a Saturday, while you are driving on an icy road 25 miles from your condominium, that the gas gauge is on empty.

5) You take up skiing after a 27-year layoff and are the only person in the quad chairlift line with leather lace-up boots, stretch pants, long thongs and a White Stag parka.

6) You are driving your van at 63 mph and nine of your pals are drinking beer in the back when you pass an unmarked, small-town police car on a two-lane road leading out of town. A few minutes later you discover that he was traveling at the posted speed limit of 35.

7) You are riding in a ski-patrol toboggan that is being steered by the prettiest lady you have ever followed down a mountain.

8) You ski into the singles line at the quad and end up riding with your ex-wife, her weekend spousal equivalent and his private jet pilot.

9) You are told by the high school age ski shop clerk that you just bought the wrong brand of shaped skis for $699.

10) You separate your skis so they won't be stolen while you have lunch and then drink so much red wine you can't remember where you put your second ski.

11) You give your wife an exclusive designed very expensive ski suit for Christmas and then see someone at breakfast in your hotel the first morning wearing the exact same outfit in the exact same color.

12) You ignore the chain law and then discover that the Highway Patrol doesn't.

13) You buy new ski boots that are supposed to be comfortable but they give you black-and-blue toes the first day of your week-long vacation.

14) You try to remember on a powder morning whether you said you would meet your wife at chair 10 at 11 or chair 11 at 10.

15) You admit that your kids are snowboarders.

16) You admit that you are a snowboarder.

17) You get to the ski resort and are unloading the car when you discover that there are only three skis on the roof: your wife's pair and one of yours.

18) You drive 300 miles to get to the parking lot of Mt. Perfect and see that part of your favorite run is covered with a narrow strip of man-made snow bordered by streams of muddy water.

19) You dress for a sunny spring day and then a blizzard arrives just as you get to the top of the mountain for your second run.

20) You buy snow tires and discover that they are useless on ice.

21) You are taking the skis off of the roof of the car when your wife says, "I need a new pair of gloves," your son sulks away with his snowboard, your daughter says she wants to take a ski lesson from that darling new instructor she met last weekend, you need to get your edges filed and they all want money from you for lunch. When you go to the ATM you discover it has run out of money on a Saturday morning and when you try to buy ski lift tickets for your family, the cashier tells you that your credit card has been declined because it is over its $10,000 limit.

The shrinks will tell you that insecurity is the real attraction of skiing. The act of hurtling yourself down a snow-covered hill within inches of trees is the real draw. And therein lies the reward for all your insecurities.

What Happened to the Entrepreneurs?

In 1936, Union Pacific Railroad president Averell Harriman created Sun Valley, Idaho, because he had enjoyed skiing in St. Anton, Austria. But there was no uphill transportation in St. Anton, and he had to climb to ski, so he had engineers invent the chairlift in his railroad yard in Omaha, Nebraska. The many different parts were designed, fabricated and transported to a remote hill near the end of a railroad spur in Ketchum, Idaho, and then hauled up the hill on the backs of mules. Five months later, just in time for Christmas, the lift carried skiers up Dollar Mountain.

In the '30s, U.S. Forest Service permits could be had for the asking and the American destination ski resort was invented. Harriman had enough capital behind him to buy 4,500 acres of land around that first chairlift so he could build a base village, too. A year later, a young snow surveyor walked into a bank in Bishop, California, and asked to borrow $84 against his Harley to buy the parts for his first rope tow. The banker initially turned him down but when he left, the banker's secretary said, "If you don't loan that nice young man that $84, I'm going to quit." The banker loaned the young entrepreneur the money, and since then Dave McCoy has personally supervised the construction of every lift on Mammoth Mountain. At one time during his more than 60-year career, Dave even owned the bank that loaned him the original $84.

In 1948, Harriman's Sun Valley decided to build a new lift on Dollar Mountain. Everett Kircher, an automobile salesman from Detroit, bought the lift, converted it into a double chairlift and put it up at Boyne Mountain, Michigan. As the story goes, Kircher bought the Boyne land for less than $100 from a farmer who couldn't grow any crops on that side of it. But it was the highest mountain in Michigan

and under Kircher's guidance, it became a huge success. Today, the Kircher family also owns Boyne Mountain; Boyne Highlands; Big Sky, Montana; Crystal Mountain, Washington; Brighton, Utah; Cypress Bowl, British Columbia; Sky Lift at Gatlinburgh, Tennessee and 10 golf courses nationwide.

In the late '30s, Wayne Poulsen and Marty Arroge bought a meadow in the Sierras for a rumored $10,000. In 1948 they sold part of it to

WARRENISM

"The best mind-altering drug is powder snow."

Alex Cushing so he could build California's first double chairlift. Alex not only built a chairlift, he started to develop a world-class resort that later would host the 1960 Winter Olympics.

About that same time, Bob Mickelsen, who was the president of the Edelweiss skiwear company, found an isolated piece of land within 50 miles of Seattle and a short distance from a six-lane freeway. I spent two days flying around in a helicopter with Jim Whitaker, the first American to summit Everest, and three or four other skiers and put together another promotional film for Bob to sell vacant lots at his potential ski resort. The first morning he showed the film in Seattle, he sold 47 lots at what later became Alpental.

In the late '50s, a veteran of the Tenth Mountain Division found the perfect place to build his dream ski resort, so he and some friends bought a ranch under the guise that they were going to start a rod and gun club. Instead, they built a ski resort and sold lots at the base to skiers. Those vacant lots sold for $5,000 and $10,000, and with each lot you got four lifetime season passes thrown in. The $20,000 homes that were built on those $5,000 lots in the '60s have sold as tear-downs recently for as much as $9 million. Pete Seibert was the entrepreneur and his dream resort became Vail, Colorado.

Throughout the '50s, '60s and '70s, major destination ski resorts were being created at the rate of about one every year or two. Then, gradually, environmental groups made the permit process impossible to cope with.

The current entrepreneurial trend is to simply buy up existing ski resorts and to homogenize them under one ownership. Entrepreneurs are moving numbers around on a financial balance sheet and selling stock instead of logging ski trails, moving dirt, putting up ski lifts and building dreams.

It has been fascinating to watch the change in attitude over the last 50 years. I used to be able to phone someone at a ski resort and ask if I could stop by and take movies to help promote their new resort in my next film. Last fall, I was looking for new things to film in the ski business. I telephoned a major ski resort in Colorado for its 218-page four-color brochure. The electronic voice that answered said, "S-p-e-l-l—y-o-u-r—n-a-m-e—a-n-d—a-d-d-r-e-s-s—s-l-o-w-l-y."

The electronic voice repeated my correct name and address and then said, "P-l-e-a-s-e—a-l-l-o-w—f-o-u-r—t-o—s-i-x—w-e-e-k-s—f-o-r—d-e-l-i-v-e-r-y."

I made that phone call in November, and I never did get the brochure. The whole experience made me appreciate the past and people like Ted Johnson, who used to flip burgers at the top of the ski lift at Alta. At the end of the day he would ski over the ridge and down into the next valley. Before long he was buying up old mining claims from little old ladies who lived in house trailers in Torrance, California, or in tract homes in Minneapolis, Minnesota. When Ted had all of the mining claims and surface rights bought up, he took a movie that I had edited for him on the road and convinced Dick Bass to fund his dream. Together they created Snowbird, Utah.

Where have all of the entrepreneurs gone? Most of them have had their spirit destroyed by the people who chain themselves to the trees when someone tries to build a new ski resort. And so you might ask yourself: What would you be doing this winter if these successful entrepreneurs had been shut down by environmentalists?

Reality Check

What is reality? Is it that incredible backlit powder shot on the January cover of your favorite ski publication? Is it that triple back flip you see Steve Stunning do on that television commercial? Can reality possibly be that wonderful four-wheel-drive, five-on-the-floor, $43,000-rebate SUV hauling skiers to the top of the mountain? Is reality the words the ski resorts use to describe their better-than-perfect ski resort?

Let's take a look:

Walking Distance To The Lift. This means: A 15-minute walk to a bus that comes every half hour that always leaves one minute before you get there. A bus that will give you a cold, bumpy 27-minute ride to the chairlift. A bus that is really a modified truck that they use to haul hogs in the summer.

Hot Water Swimming Pool Adjacent To The Lodge. Reality will reveal a jacuzzi large enough for a cocker spaniel to swim laps in. If you don't get into the hot water within 30 minutes of when they take the cover off, the water won't be hot.

Modest Prices In Our Deluxe Mountaintop Restaurant. Be sure to bring your own tuna fish sandwiches, because at the Summit House they cost $9.95 each. A cup of coffee is $3.75. A $12.75 hamburger will reveal where they filmed that famous television commercial, "Where's the beef?"

MOUNT PERFECT MOUNTAINTOP RESTAURANT

Sandwiches
Hamburger --- $12.75
Grilled Cheese -- $9.95
Tuna --- $9.95
Combo --- $14.95
Peanut Butter and Jelly ------------------------------------ $6.95
Cheeseburger --- $14.95
Patty Melt -- $10.95
PIZZA
By the slice --- $7.95
Plus each type of topping add ----------------------------- $2.00
DRINKS
Beer Domestic by the bottle ------------------------------- $3.95
     Tap -- $4.95
     Imported --- $5.95
Soft drinks -- $2.95
Milk shakes --- $4.95
Smoothies -- $6.95
FRESH FRUIT
Bananas -- $2.95
Apples -- $1.95
PASTRIES
Chocolate Chip cookies ------------------------------------ $3.95
Pie by the slice -- $3.95

*Notice: Any parties larger than two, will have
An 18% gratuity added to their bill*

Airport Nearby. This means that the bus that takes you from the airport to the resort has a bathroom in it. That's because it stops at all 19 towns en route to deliver mail, pick up the milk and drop off parcels. But you'll be in luck as it will be driven by a recent Russian immigrant who spent the last five years driving a dump truck at the copper mine in Siberia, so he is used to icy roads.

All-Weather Highway. Reality will show that, when it snows, our highly skilled staff of skid chain installers will be happy to put your chains on your car for only $20. This is the same happy staff that puts out the skid chain control sign as soon as the snow gets as deep as a quarter of an inch.

Sports Center. In reality, this torture center was designed to be used when the snow is icy, which it usually is. That's because the head of the snowmaking department is a major stockholder in the sports center.

The sports center charges you $30 a day to do the same exercises you can do at your local YMCA for only $4, and that's without driving 500 miles to do it. Plus $30 to play at racquetball, aerobics, dancercise, weights, paddle tennis or swimming. After your workout, there is a health food bar where you can buy a sprout salad that offers you a choice of seven different kinds of lettuce. And the salad is only $11.75. Towels and lockers are extra.

Comfortable Rooms With Fireplace. When the smog alert on your mantel flashes and the alarm goes off, you'll have five minutes to douse your cozy little fire. If you don't put out the fire within the allotted time period, you will be billed an extra $200, which is exactly twice what the pollution control officer will fine the condo owners when they see the smoke still coming out of your numbered and registered chimney.

Tea Dancing. Reality means that the strobe lighting will make your sunburned eyes feel better because it is only bright half the time. The music is at the same decibel level as the roar in Mile High Stadium when the Broncos score a touchdown. The waitress has to serve so many tables that whatever it was on the rocks you ordered will be whatever you ordered and warm water by the time she gets it to you.

WARRENISM

"Time is a great teacher, but it eventually kills all its pupils."

Accurate Trail Maps. In reality, trail maps are designed to provide a view as if you were in a helicopter above the parking lot. Once the artwork is done, it is reduced to the size of a postage stamp so the resort can sell advertising around the edges to pay for the artist's trip to Europe. At the top of the hill, reality makes you turn the map upside down. All the trail names are now upside down and impossible to read. "Dead Man's Dive" becomes "Evid S'nam Daed." Your new lady friend bets you a steak dinner "Evid S'nam Daed" is to the left as you look down. Two hours later you find that you have just negotiated "Noynac Htaed."

The Good Old Days

s the quad chairlift cleared the loading ramp and accelerated to 1,100 feet a minute, we lowered the foot rest and the fellow sitting next to me said, "Look at all them snowboarders down there! Skiing sure wasn't like this in the good old days."

By the looks of his ski gear, he spoke from experience. He wore tight, faded navy blue bell-bottom stretch pants, a pair of Henke boots, a faded navy blue and Chinese red Sportcaster hip-length quilted parka and K2 Cheesburger skis with Cubco bindings. This guy had been making the scene since before there was a scene.

But his comment started me thinking. Just how good were the good old days?

Most of the things we take for granted today had not been invented when Ward Baker and I spent the winter of 1946-47 living in the Sun Valley, Idaho, parking lot. The good thing about living there for three and a half months in an eight-foot trailer was that we skied every day for 18 cents a day.

But I get ahead of myself.

Here are a few of the things we didn't have in those good old days.

Safety bindings (or release bindings, as they are called today)? No way. When you fell, your skis stayed on, and your leg sometimes fell off. Or at least it revolved, independent of your torso.

Plastic ski boots? Didn't exist. We wore soft leather boots that reached only as high as our ankle bones. Today those boots wouldn't even be considered enough support for cross-country skiing.

Thermal long underwear? Nope. Our long johns were made of wool, and when they got wet they itched so badly you could hardly sit still on the chairlift.

Waterproof ski clothes? Forget it. Not even a nylon parka existed then, much less an insulated, quilted nylon parka.

Metal or fiberglass skis? No such thing. Everyone skied on stiff hickory boards that were so long they reached to your outstretched hand held high over your head. Unless your skis were seven-feet, six-inches long, you were considered a wimp.

Grooming machinery? Forget that. Racers sidestepped down a slalom or downhill course to pack and smooth it the day before the race. Otherwise, you skied the snow in whatever condition you found it. The moguls just got bigger and bigger until a snowstorm filled them in.

Snow tires? Never heard of them. Skid chains cost $4.95 a pair and took an hour and a half to put on. You did this while lying on your back in the mud in a roadside parking area just below the altitude where the rain turned to snow.

Quad chairlifts? Nope. They didn't even have double chairlifts until 1949. All the chairs were single. You rode all alone in the wind and snow and rain. There was no way to cozy up to that ski companion of your dreams. When the lift broke, which it did often, you hoped you were close enough to the ground to take off your skis and jump. Otherwise you just sat there and froze until they somehow got the lift running again before nightfall.

High-speed lifts? No way. Most ski resorts only had one single chairlift. It carried about 400 people an hour, and on most weekends the liftline was over half an hour long.

Your choice of hundreds of ski resorts? Not a chance. Here's a few ski resorts that didn't exist in 1946: Squaw Valley, Heavenly Valley, Whistler, Vail, Sugarbush, Snowbird, Crystal Mountain, Copper Mountain, Keystone, Breckenridge, Jackson Hole, Mt. Snow, Killington, Stratton, Waterville Valley, Boyne Mountain, Park City, Deer Valley, Taos, Big Sky and Crested Butte. But pioneers here and there were putting up ropetows with a couple of thousand feet of navy surplus rope, a few sheaves nailed to trees and an old car to power it. A ropetow, an outhouse and a muddy parking lot were the amenities available. You ate your peanut butter sandwich in your car and, if you knew someone who was rich, they might rent a motel for $5 a night.

Entertainment? After going to the 25-cent movie in town, the rich friend might sneak your carload of friends and their sleeping bags into the motel and let them sleep on the floor for 50 cents a body.

Rent a condo? Not invented yet. All the rooms in Sun Valley, Idaho, slept 846 people in 1946. If you were good with tools, you remodeled the back seat of your car so you could sleep in it and cook your meals over a Coleman stove. In 1954, Ed's Beds would come on the scene in Aspen at $3 a night.

Interstate highways? Forget it. The drive from Denver to Aspen was a seven- or eight-hours on a snow- and ice-covered two-land road, up over 13,000-foot Loveland Pass and then 11,000-foot Vail Pass.

Getting stuck behind an 18-wheeler crawling over the pass at five or six miles an hour was normal.

Check your skis on your flight? No way! In 1952, the first few times I flew, they had to slide my skis under the three back seats of the DC-3. Flying from Los Angeles to Europe involved staying overnight in New York after the eight-hour first leg of the trip. Then New York to Newfoundland to Scotland, with the navigator of the DC-6 taking occasional star sights with a sextant to rediscover where we were in relation to where we were supposed to be.

In the good old days, you got to drive narrow, icy roads without snow tires, power brakes, power steering, automatic transmission or four-wheel drive. Of course, gasoline only cost 20 cents a gallon.

In the good old days, you got to stand in 45-minute liftlines with itchy, wet long underwear because your gabardine ski pants weren't waterproof. You got to feel the water seep in through the holes in your lace-up ski boots. You got to peer through foggy goggles as the ski patrol hauled another skier off the hill with a spiral fracture caused by the lack of safety bindings.

So give me skiing as it is today, on a run that was groomed to corduroy perfection the night before, riding up the mountain on a high-speed quad lift while dressed comfortably in layers of waterproof-breathable clothing, plastic boots with heaters, thermal socks and underwear that wicks away sweat, insulated gloves, fog-free goggles, release bindings tuned to my weight and ability, lightweight pencil-thin poles and a pair of soft-flexing fat skis to carve up yet another untracked powder slope.

I started making turns in 1937 on a pair of $2 pine skis with leather toe straps. Since then, fortunately, the inventors of ski stuff have kept ahead of my need for equipment that makes the sport easier on my body.

For me every day is a good old day, and each day is better than the last.

I'm Warren Miller, and I hope to see you same time, same place as I continue my lifelong search for the free lift ticket.

WARREN MILLER
APRIL 1948

.

WARREN MILLER
4 – 1948

Other Warren Miller Books

"You have enjoyed his ski movies for years. Now enjoy his hilarious books about those years."

W arren began filming skiing in 1949, when there were less than 15 chairlifts in North America and tickets cost as much as four dollars a day. Since 1946 he's been writing and drawing cartoons about the good and bad days of skiing. Now you can order any or all of his humorous, best-selling books.

Order all five of them, and they will even arrive autographed. Mail, fax, or email and charge your order to your Visa or Mastercard. Send to MAC productions, P.O. Box 84, Duvall, WA 98019 Fax: 425-844-9245 or email: mac.productions@gte.net Add $5.00 for shipping and handling of first book, $2.00 for each additional book. Allow two weeks for delivery.

On Film in Print

Warren has been skiing and surfing since 1937 and has spent most of the last 50 years on the road with his camera and skis, boats and windsurfers, while chasing freedom, finding it, filming it, or writing about it. This is a collection of almost 50 short stories about his unusual lifestyle while traveling the world from New Zealand to Zermatt, from Malibu to Maui and a lot of other places in between.

ITEM #301 Soft Cover $12.95
ITEM #302 Hard Cover $24.95

A Nose for Wine

Warren's irreverent cartoon illustrations of wine-speak. "Great legs," "Tannin," "A hint of bitterness," "Well proportioned" are just a few of the misunderstood wine terms that are explained by Jeannie McGill and humorously illustrated by Warren.

ITEM #601 Hard Cover $19.95

ITEM #501 Soft Cover $11.95

Wine, Women, Warren, & Skis

The hilarious saga of Warren's six-month ski trip during the winter of '46-'47 while living on oyster crackers and ketchup, frozen rabbits, poached ducks, goat meat, and powder snow. He slept in an eight-foot trailer at eight below zero in the finest ski resort parking lots in the West. Learn how to ski for a hundred days in Sun Valley, Idaho, for only $18 or at Alta, Utah, for $2.50 a week. And there are a lot of antique photos to prove it.

Ski and Snow Country

120 brilliant black-and-white photographs by Ray Atkeson from the 1940s and '50s with an essay and captions by Warren Miller. Almost everyone in the book was a friend of Warren's, so he wrote it the same way he used to narrate his movies, with a combination of nostalgia, reportage and humor. For anyone who skied, or had a friend or relative who skied in the formative years of the sport, this is a coffee-table book designed for you.

ITEM #201 Hard Cover $23.95

Lurching from One Near Disaster to the Next

A collection of 50 short stories from the last 50 years of Warren lurching through life. The Truck from Hell, Golf Anyone, The Whirlpool and Swimming with the Whales are just some of the classic stories in this, the latest collection of stories about Warren's unique lifestyle.

ITEM #401 Soft Cover $14.95
ITEM #402 Hard Cover $24.95